WEBB SOCIETY DEEP-SKY OBSERVER'S HANDBOOK

VOLUME 6
ANONYMOUS GALAXIES

WEBB SOCIETY DEEP-SKY OBSERVER'S HANDBOOK

VOLUME 6
ANONYMOUS GALAXIES

Compiled by the Webb Society
Edited by Kenneth Glyn Jones, F.R.A.S.
Written and illustrated by Malcolm J. Thomson and
Ronald J. Morales

With a foreword by Walter Scott Houston
(Joseph Meek Observatory)

ENSLOW PUBLISHERS, INC.

Bloy St. & Ramsey Ave.	P.O. Box 38
Box 777	Aldershot
Hillside, N.J. 07205	Hants GU12 6BP
U.S.A.	U.K.

Library of Congress Cataloging in Publication Data
(Revised for vol. 6-7)

Webb Society deep-sky observer's handbook.

First published under title: The Webb Society
observers handbook, 1975-   .
Vols. 6-   : published by Enslow Publishers,
Hillside, N.J.
Includes bibliographies.
Contents: v. 1. Double stars — v. 2. Planetary
and gaseous nebulae — v. 3. Open and globular
clusters — v. 4. Galaxies — v. 5. Clusters of
galaxies — v. 6. Anonymous galaxies — v. 7.
The Southern sky.
1. Astronomy—Observers' manuals. I. Jones,
Kenneth Glyn. II. Webb Society. III. Title.
QB64.W36 1979   523.8'9   78-31260
ISBN 0-89490-027-7 (v. 1)

Printed in the United States of America

10 9 8 7 6 5 4 3 2

To Walter Scott Houston,
Doyen of Deep-Sky Observers,
With gratitude and affection.

CONTENTS

LIST OF ILLUSTRATIONS

FOREWORD

Incredibly, and almost without warning, the frontiers of amateur astronomy in the last fifteen years have been pushed back by millions of light-years. Some variable star observers will not now estimate variables brighter than 13th magnitude. Ordinary amateurs purchase copy sheets of the Palomar Atlas because even the BD, SAO and AAVSO atlases go only to magnitude 9.5. O'Meara, with a 24-inch atop a volcano in Hawaii, and sucking oxygen in the thin air, is detecting visually stars below the plate levels of the Palomar atlas. My mail is full of requests to identify faint nebulae which the amateur cannot find in the NGC.

The absurd 12-inch aperture limit that had restricted telescope size for so long crumpled before the simple support system of the Dobsonian mounting, and Teflon bearings eliminated the expensive and cumbersome mountings that had previously dominated the field. Now, in this new volume of the Webb Society Deep-Sky Observer's Handbook, there is an exciting beginning, a new-age travel guide to the faint, further domains of our Universe.

This book will inspire serious amateurs world-wide, and it will delight historians of science because it maps paths into the future. The authors are Malcolm J. Thomson and Ronald J. Morales, both masterly observers who also have their own fair share of genius, as this volume attests. To provide a guide for the new generation of amateurs they used scopes of 13.1-inch, 16.5-inch and 17.5-inch aperture to break the grip of the NGC which has bound amateurs for over a century. What they did was to observe carefully some 165 faint, uncatalogued - and so 'anonymous' galaxies. They wrote meticulous descriptions, did drawings of some, made notes of curious things they saw, and produced a manual on how to hunt down these strangers of the skies. The amateur with a big telescope who found previous guide books no test of either himself or his optics now has a task worthy of his powers.

This is not all: besides being a guide to the hitherto unexplored, the book is important as an historical and symbolic entity. It keeps alight the power of amateur astronomy which has so helped to guide and sustain professional astronomy over three centuries and more. If this sounds an extravagant claim, hear this:

Lewis Epstein, professional physicist and amateur astronomer, speaking at the Astronomical Society of the Pacific, put it this way with deft precision:

"the most valuable thing amateur astronomers do is to plant and cultivate the seed for the next generation of professionals - professional

physicists, mathematicians and engineers as well as professional
astronomers".

Essentially the same message came to me from Harlow Shapley in 1931
when he came to Milwaukee Astronomical Society - a 'free' talk - to all 15
of us. Shapley declared that amateurs were most important, and justified
it this way:

"In the past, astronomy has survived on bequests by rich men. They
have other uses for their money now. Astronomy must now depend on
government funding, and the amounts will depend on the attitude and
interests of the general public which will control events for many years.
Amateurs will help set these attitudes of the voters. My attitudes on
this are most unpopular at Harvard: if I did not hold a Chair, my stay
there might be quite short". (Paraphrase from my notes).

Fifty years apart, yet Shapley felt the same way that Epstein does
today. To Shapley, the responsibility for the future of astronomy, for its
health and well-being, was not to be entrusted to college Dons, nor to the
media, but to the mere existence of amateur astronomers as the group best
qualified to preserve the essential structure of the science. Perhaps
David Levy also understood when he said: "If we don't get the children
interested, there'll be no next generation of astronomers".

All this may seem a long way removed from the purpose of 'Anonymous
Galaxies', but that is decidedly not the case. Astronomy needs the
amateur in more ways than variable star observations or meteor counting.
The social role of the non-professional observer looks more essential than
ever. But the amateur can use a certain amount of initial direction. He
needs a push he never realises. T.W. Webb's 'Celestial Objects for Common
Telescopes' did just that more than a hundred years ago: we know the
results.

But since Webb - and Admiral Smyth - there has been a great dearth of
such support. Many writers of popular books have borrowed from Webb, but
none exploited the psychological gains that Webb created. It took over a
century for a true successor to appear in the guise of the Webb Society's
'Handbooks': to bring valid inspiration, a new vigour to direct the
amateur towards targets well beyond the year 2000. This is what this
volume will do. The observers who use it may not reflect upon any larger
social purpose, but they will nevertheless be doing the things so
symbiotic and so necessary to all astronomy.

Walter Scott Houston
The Joseph Meek Observatory
East Haddam
Connecticut 06423

GENERAL PREFACE

Named after the Rev. T.W. Webb (1807 - 1885), an eminent amateur astronomer and author of the classic <u>Celestial Objects for Common Telescopes</u>, the Webb Society exists to encourage the study of double stars and deep-sky objects. It has members in almost every country where amateur astronomy flourishes. It has a number of Observing Sections, each organised by a director with wide experience in the particular field, the main ones being Double Stars, Nebulae & Clusters, Galaxies and Southern Sky. Publications include a Quarterly Journal containing articles, special features, book reviews and section reports that cover the society's activities. Membership is open to anyone whose interests are compatible. Enquiries and membership applications can be sent to the Secretary: Steven J. Hynes, 8 Cormorant Close, Sydney, Crewe, Cheshire CW1 1LN, England, or to the North America Secretary: Ronald J. Morales, 1440 South Marmora, Tucson, Arizona 85713-1015, U.S.A.

Webb's <u>Celestial Objects for Common Telescopes</u>, first published in 1859, must have been among the most popular books of its kind ever written. Running through six editions by 1917, it is still in print although the text is of more historical than practical interest to the amateur of today. Not only has knowledge of the Universe been transformed by modern developments, but the present generation of amateur astronomers has telescopes and other equipment that even the professional of Webb's day would have envied.

The aim of the new <u>Webb Society Deep-Sky Observer's Handbook</u> is to provide a series of observer's manuals that do justice to the equipment that is available today and to cover fields that have not been adequately covered by other organisations of amateurs. We have tried to make these guides the best of their kind: they are written by experts, some of them professional astronomers, who have had considerable practical experience with the pleasures and problems of the amateur astronomer. The manuals can be used profitably by beginners, who will find much to stimulate their enthusiasm and imagination. However, they are designed primarily for the more experienced amateur who seeks greater scope for the exercise of his skills.

Each handbook is complete with regard to its subject. The reader is given an adequate historical and theoretical basis for a modern understanding of the physical role of the objects covered in the wider context of the Universe. He is provided with a thorough exposition of observing methods, including the construction and operation of ancillary equipment such as micrometers and simple spectroscopes. Each volume contains a detailed and comprehensive catalogue of objects for the amateur to locate and to observe with an eye made more perceptive by the knowledge he has gained.

We hope that these volumes will enable the reader to extend his abilities, to exploit his telescope to its limit, and to tackle the challenging difficulties of new fields of observation with confidence of success.

EDITOR'S PREFACE
VOLUME 6: ANONYMOUS GALAXIES

With the publication of this volume we introduce the amateur deep-sky observer to what must be the ultimate in astronomical adventure and discovery. Anonymous galaxies are objects which are 'unknown' even to that comprehensive compilation, the New General Catalogue and its two Index supplements. In order to observe and identify objects which eluded the acuity of William and John Herschel and their successors in visual discovery, the modern amateur observer needs to extend his ability and his instruments to the limit. Nevertheless, the scope for successful work in this field, if exacting, is also virtually limitless, and it is the purpose of this book to explain and demonstrate how that success can most efficiently be achieved.

After a brief historical review, the text of Part One describes in detail the older visual catalogues and the many modern photographic catalogues and atlases upon which the search for anonymous galaxies must be based. In following chapters, the methodology and discipline required to observe such faint and remote objects provides a thorough training for the eye and the mind, and for which the whole of Part One is an indispensable guide.

In Part Two, the Catalogue with its detailed locating diagrams covers the original observation of 165 galaxies: many of these are listed in one or other of the specialised catalogues, but some are 'unlisted' or truly anonymous galaxies, of which the authors can claim unique 'discovery'.

The telescopes used in this survey range from 13.1-inch (33 cm.) to 17½-inch (44 cm.), which nowadays can be considered as only moderate apertures for the keen amateur astronomer. One could, in fact, make a successful beginning in this field with any good telescope of 12-inches (30 cm.) or more, but of course the greater the aperture employed the greater will be the number of anonymous galaxies accessible to detection.

Apart from the satisfaction of exercising one's skill to the utmost in picking up some - or all - of the objects listed and depicted here, the greatest thrill must be the occasion when one locates and identifies a completely new and 'unlisted' object for oneself. In such a case - to be the first and only person to have observed that object visually - is truly a unique feat of discovery!

With the object of encouraging more interest in this new-age exploration of the deep skies, the Webb Society has initiated the formation of an Anonymous Galaxies Club, details of which are given in Appendix 1. Any observer who wishes to contribute the results of his explorations in this field is welcome to take up membership in what is likely to be a very prestigious band of enthusiasts.

The authors of this book are amateur astronomers of wide experience in all aspects of their craft, and in the field of observing anonymous galaxies they are truly pioneers.

Malcolm J. Thomson was born in Plymouth, England in 1933, but in 1950 paid a visit to California - and stayed there for 34 years. He now enjoys a happy retirement with his wife in Mexico. His early interest in astronomy flourished in the generous Californian climate, and being invited to use the 16½-inch reflector of Westmont College Observatory, he exploited the opportunity to the full. His unique talents led him to the exploration of the fainter NGC galaxies and to the solving of many existing problems of identification. His outstanding contributions to the W.S.Q.J. in this field gained him the Webb Society Award in 1976, and this present volume is a further demonstration of his abilities.

Ronald J. Morales, born in Queens, New York, in 1946, had an early interest in science which led him to the Junior Curatorship in Science at the Brooklyn Children's Museum for the years 1960-64. In 1965 he joined the U.S. Marines for four years, during which he attained the rank of sergeant, served in Vietnam, and was awarded the Navy Achievement Medal in combat. On moving to Tucson, Arizona in 1972 he set up his first observatory and was soon contributing a 'Deep Sky Vistas' column in both 'Star and Sky' and 'Popular Astronomy' magazines. Membership of the Webb Society gave him further opportunity to communicate his ideas, and soon led to his receiving the Webb Society Award in 1983. The clear skies of the Sonoran Desert, where he has established an observatory, allow him to exercise his outstanding skill as a deep-sky observer for the benefit of us all.

The Editor and the Webb Society Committee are deeply indebted to these two outstanding observers for the sustained effort required to compile this volume which now stands as a tribute to their search for excellence. Our thanks, too, are due to our Secretary, Steve Hynes, for his long and patient work in producing the finished copy of both text and illustrations.

To Walter Scott Houston, who has honoured us by accepting the dedication of this volume, we offer our respect and gratitude. He is, of course, well known to many thousands of perceptive astronomers throughout the world for his eagerly read 'Deep Sky Wonders' column in 'Sky & Telescope'. His interests in astronomy are wide-ranging and as his generous Foreword to this book shows, he is one of those far-sighted commentators who really understands where the future of amateur astronomy lies. In following his lead we shall not only be guided by sound principles, but we may also learn to guide our successors in the same direction.

Authors' Acknowledgements

Great credit is due to Ms. Cindy Mills (typing) and Ms. Ann Stenz (proof-reading) for their expert execution of these vital tasks.

PART ONE

THE OBSERVATION
OF
ANONYMOUS GALAXIES

1. INTRODUCTION AND HISTORICAL REVIEW

The term 'anonymous galaxies' refers to any galaxy not included in either the New General Catalogue (NGC) or the two Index Catalogues (IC I and IC II). All of the NGC and most of the IC I galaxies were discovered visually prior to the twentieth century whilst those listed in IC II were for the most part discovered photographically. Thus, with the publication in 1908 of the IC II, the pre-anonymous listing of galaxies was complete, and those discovered subsequently are therefore included in the classification of anonymous galaxies.

Shortly after 1908 it was apparent to the investigators of nebulae that a great number of additional objects existed, but these were generally ignored for individual study because the brighter and larger objects, listed in the NGC and IC catalogues, offered more opportunity of producing results to those conducting telescopic studies in this field.

In 1918, H.B. Curtis produced a notable paper which was published as part of Vol. XIII of the Lick Observatory Publications, in which he described the appearance of some 762 nebulae and star clusters. All of the nebulae, which would today fall into the category of galaxies, were objects already included in either the NGC or IC, but Curtis made it a point in his paper to note that numbers of additional galaxies were visible on his study plates. These he described only as 'S.N.' or 'small nebulae': nevertheless it was at least an early recognition that vast numbers of galaxies existed beyond those listed in the NGC and IC.

For many years these small, fainter galaxies received scant attention, and it was not until after the completion of the Palomar Observatory Sky Survey in 1956 that subsequent study of these prints revealed for the first time the immense number of uncatalogued galaxies which populated the observable universe. The world-wide distribution of this photographic catalogue to leading astronomical institutions resulted in the publication of updated catalogues covering the various different types of deep-sky objects. Three of these new catalogues concerned themselves solely with galaxies and each of them, for the first time, listed thousands of new or 'anonymous' galaxies.

In order of date of publication these catalogues are:

1. Morphological Catalogue of Galaxies. 4 Volumes, University of Moscow, 1964, by Prof. B.A. Vorontsov-Velyaminov and V.P. Arhipova. Contains about 29,000 galaxies north of Declination -33°.

2. Catalogue of Galaxies and Clusters of Galaxies. 6 Volumes, California Institute of Technology, Pasadena, 1961-1968, by Prof. F. Zwicky et al.

Introduction

This lists 31,350 galaxies down to photographic magnitude (Mp) 15.5.

3. <u>Uppsala General Catalogue of Galaxies.</u> Uppsala, 1973, by P. Nilson.
Records 12,921 galaxies north of Declination $-2\frac{1}{2}$.

These catalogues will be more fully described in Chapter 2.

All of the catalogues mentioned above provide valuable information to
any observer interested in anonymous galaxies studies, but it should be
pointed out that anyone deciding to enter this field of observation should
endeavour to obtain access to a copy of the Palomar Observatory Sky Survey
(generally available at any University or Astronomical Institution library).

Access to the Palomar Survey prints is important because, when visually
observing any field containing more than one galaxy, it is very easy to
mis-identify the visible nebular images. Only by examining and using
measurements on the relevant print in conjunction with one of the above
mentioned catalogues, can correct identification be made.

Now let us examine the basic requirements necessary for conducting a
successful programme of observing anonymous galaxies. Due to the fact that
most anonymous galaxies are fainter than Mp 13.0, one generally requires a
telescope of at least 10-inches aperture. It is also very important that
the observer is proficient in using medium to high powers of magnification.
In order to successfully recognise many faint and small nebular images as
something other than stars, it is often vital to employ the highest
magnification available. Many faint small elliptical galaxies which cannot
be distinguished as such with x84 or x176 become quite obvious with powers
of x350 or x420.

Personal Experience (MJT):

The visual study of anonymous galaxies, by its very nature, is bound to
be attended by some initial trials and disappointments, and it may be
helpful to the reader to share, vicariously, those of one of the authors of
this book.

My own experience shows that on any average night the percentage of
successful observations is usually below 50%; thus a large proportion of
observing time is spent fruitlessly searching fields which produce only
negative results. However, on those other, successful occasions, it is a
great boost to morale to know that the probability is high that you are the
first observer actually to see the sought for object. Thus, in one sense,
you become the visual discoverer, and acquire a new-found status thereby.

The first anonymous galaxy I actually observed was U 02126, which at

Introduction

that time, November 1974, and for many months following, I believed was
an observation of NGC 1003. This was before I had access to either of the
three major catalogues or the Palomar prints, and my error highlights the
necessity to consult such references in order to identify correctly such
faint galaxies.

In January 1975, while observing the field containing the galaxies NGC
3073 and NGC 3079, I noted a third nebular image north - preceding NGC 3079.
Follow-up investigation proved this object to be neither an NGC nor an IC
nebula and eventually I was able to determine that it was the anonymous
galaxy MCG 9-17-9. The excitement of this observation led me to begin a
separate observational programme at Westmont College Observatory,
resulting in my own 'Visual Survey of Anonymous Galaxies'. Since that
initial recognised discovery I have used the Uppsala Catalogue as my main
source of reference in searching for anonymous galaxies and have so far
(October 1984) recorded observations of 137 of these objects. Results of
this work have been published in various issues of the Webb Society
Quarterly Journal (W.S.Q.J.).

Certainly the search has been personally gratifying, especially as the
results have all been obtained with a telescope of 16½-inch aperture.
This leads me to believe that many amateurs restrict their observing
programmes to limitations below the capabilities of their telescopes.

At this point it may be useful to make some general comments about
observing conditions - these concern my own locality of course, but some
will apply to those faced by many amateurs.

Santa Barbara does not have particularly transparent skies although
seeing conditions are generally quite good. Therefore, in order to
achieve the best possible results, it is important to adhere to certain
methods. Almost all observing is conducted after midnight in order to
lessen the artificial light pollution experienced with all cities. In
addition, most observations are carried out when the object lies within
one hour of the meridian, thus obtaining the brightest image possible.
By following these two procedures I have been able to observe quite
successfully galaxies listed as faint as Mp 16.0.

Observation of anonymous galaxies is not an easy programme to carry
out, but to the visual astronomer who seeks a challenge which will require
all his observing skills, coupled with the pushing of his telescope to its
limits, it can be both fulfilling and exciting, to say nothing of the
additional thrill of original visual discovery.

Introduction

The Westmont Telescope

The 16½-inch reflecting telescope of the Westmont College Observatory, located in the foothills of the Santa Inez Mountains, north of Santa Barbara, California, is an ideal instrument for the visual survey of anonymous galaxies down to Mp 16.0. The telescope has an extremely stable fork type mount and is completely electrically operated, having two separate motions for R.A. drive and a single one for Declination. It can be operated either as a Newtonian, with a focal ratio of f/5, or as a Cassegrain, where the focal ratio is f/20. The tube is of the open frame type, similar to the 100-inch Mount Wilson reflector.

Slow motion controls for both R.A. and Dec. are electrically operated by a press-button panel easily accessible to the observer at either focus. Attached to the main telescope is a 5-inch short focus refractor which can be employed as either a finder or a guide scope. The setting circles are large and easily legible; the R.A. circle being divided into 4-minute intervals and the Declination circle into degrees.

For the anonymous galaxy survey I use five Plossl oculars which, when used at the Newtonian focus, provide magnifications of x84, x176, x351, x422 and x527, and I make it a point to try to observe all objects with as many of these oculars as possible. Many anonymous galaxies are small elliptical systems, often requiring x176 or x351 to provide images of sufficient size to distinguish them from faint stellar sources.

Observing Procedures

For those readers who have not yet experienced the thrill of finding their first anonymous galaxy, I propose to describe, step by step, what may be expected during a typical search, using in this example the Uppsala galaxy U 01194, R.A. 22h. 18.6m., Dec. +33° 03' (1950).

Having located the correct field in the eyepiece, I begin my observation always with the x84 eyepiece. The field is searched diligently, starting at the centre and gradually working towards the edge. This may take up to ten minutes as the eye becomes more fully dark-adapted. In this particular case I fail to detect any nebular image with x84, so I insert the x176 ocular and begin again at the centre of the field.

At this point perhaps I should admit that when dealing with extremely faint extended images, one may often sense (and I can use only this term to describe adequately the actual experience) the presence of the sought for object. This ability is acquired only by long experience in deep-sky observing: I have often examined a field with fairly low power, and been

Introduction

drawn towards a particular, virtually stellar, image, which upon
subjection to higher magnification, has revealed itself to be a galaxy.

Now back to U 01194: at x176 I can detect an extremely faint nebular
image close to the centre of the field. It is small, but shows an
extended form, elongated N.p.-S.f., and is of uniform surface brightness,
no nucleus being visible. It lies in a field in which all the closest
stars are faint: it is contained between two stars which are aligned S.p.-
N.f., the preceding star forming a triangle with two others (it is most
important to define the position of the object relative to nearby stars as
this provides a valuable reference for correct identification).

The observation continues: the galaxy is still visible with x351; it
appears to be quite narrow, like a small streak of light. It is still
visible with x427 but no additional details can be made out.

Having completed the visual description I take the earliest
opportunity to consult the relevant Palomar print in order to verify that
I have, indeed, observed the correct object. Having done so, I write up
the observation in my log book, adding any additional information about
the object which I can obtain from the appropriate catalogue. In this
case the Uppsala General Catalogue provides the following:

Uppsala U 01194, Type Sb-c (2'.5 x 0'.3). P.A. 122°, Mp 15.0
MCG 5-52-012, Fbc, A, Mp 14.0; CGCG, Anon., Mp 15.0

Conclusion

For anyone possessing the right telescopic equipment, who is prepared to
push the limits of observation beyond those of the majority, this field
is exceptional, and almost any success will lead to virtual visual
discovery. I have observed some 137 anonymous galaxies, but these are
equivalent to no more than a few grains of sand taken from the beach: the
field is wide open to anyone who really wishes to explore it.

....

2. EARLY CATALOGUES OF GALAXIES

The first catalogue of deep-sky objects to produce a significant number of galaxies was compiled in the latter half of the eighteenth century by the Frenchman Charles Messier, who, between the years 1771 and 1784, published a series of lists totalling 103 'Nebulae and Star Clusters'. Of these 103 objects we now know that some 34 of them were 'galaxies', but at that time, their extra-galactic status was hardly even guessed at. For many years the 'nebulous objects', as apart from recognised star clusters, were first of all subdivided into the 'white' and 'green' categories. Even after some of the 'white' nebulae were discovered to exhibit spiral structure in 1851, it was another 73 years before they were finally recognised as being remote systems of stars; 'island universes' or 'galaxies'.

Soon after Messier's final list was published, William Herschel in England began his surveys of the heavens, which over the next four decades, were to produce discoveries in the number of deep-sky objects far beyond those of his predecessors. Herschel used telescopes of his own design and construction to embark upon a systematic survey of the heavens, and this aspect of his work was published in three separate lists in 1786, 1789 and 1802. In total they contained descriptions of some 2500 objects, of which about 2100 are now known to be galaxies.

William Herschel is generally recognised to have been the greatest of all visual observers, and he passed on much of his outstanding ability to his son John, whose first major contribution was a survey conducted with an $18\frac{3}{4}$-inch aperture reflector mounted at the family home in Slough.

This survey, carried out between 1825 and 1833, primarily re-examined many of his father's original discoveries but in addition, John Herschel added about 500 new objects of which, again, the majority were galaxies. The results of this work were published in the 'Philosophical Transactions' of the Royal Society for 1833. In this work, John Herschel broke away from his father's method of recording an object's position by differences in R.A. and Dec. from a reference star, to giving its full co-ordinates, although he did favour the later discarded North Polar Distance when computing declination. The visual descriptions given in John Herschel's 'Observations of Nebulae and Clusters of Stars' were to set the style for most observers who followed and they are, indeed, still in use today.

During the years 1834 to 1838, John Herschel extended his survey to cover the southern hemisphere by taking his favourite $18\frac{3}{4}$-inch reflector to a site just north of Cape Town, South Africa, where he carried out the most extensive observations ever made of the southern skies. On his return to England he set about the immense task of reducing his 'Cape

Early Catalogues

Observations' for publication, which appeared in a beautiful edition in
1847, containing about 1700 objects of which almost all were new
discoveries.

By this time many new observers were becoming involved in this branch
of observational astronomy so that in the next fifty years the number of
newly discovered deep-sky objects was to multiply tremendously. Again,
the majority of these new discoveries would eventually be recognised as
belonging to that class which today we would call galaxies. Even by the
middle of the nineteenth century, John Herschel began to realise that due
to the great increase in newly discovered objects, a new, comprehensive
listing was urgently required, and it was this task he now undertook.

The 'General Catalogue of Nebulae and Clusters of Stars' was eventually
published in 1864: it listed some 5079 entries and was to remain the prime
reference work in this field until being replaced, some 30 years later, by
J.L.E. Dreyer's catalogue. By this time, interest in this branch of
observational astronomy had grown and spread in both Europe and America.
This fact, together with the increase in telescopes of both larger aperture
and improved optical quality, resulted in even greater increases in the
number of newly found deep-sky objects.

Among those engaged in this expansion of the frontiers of astronomy was
H.L. D'Arrest who carried out extremely accurate observations, mainly with
an 11-inch refractor, at Copenhagen. The results were published in 1867
under the title 'Siderum Nebulosorum', and his position measurements of
many objects provided corrections for a number of errors found in
Herschel's 'General Catalogue'.

In 1848 the Earl of Rosse completed the construction of a 72-inch
aperture reflector at his estate in Parsonstown, Ireland, the largest
telescope ever built to that time and not to be surpassed in size until the
100-inch Mt. Wilson instrument was completed nearly 70 years later. With
the 'Leviathan of Parsonstown', the observers there began a wide review of
the objects listed in the 'General Catalogue'. They soon noted that many
new objects were visible in the same fields of view containing G.C. objects,
and nearly all were later found to be galaxies. In addition to this, the
72-inch telescope revealed to the observers that some structure could be
made out in the nebulae, and that several of them displayed a spiral form,
giving rise to the significant classification, 'spiral nebulae'.

The observations carried out with the 72-inch telescope over a 30 year
period were collated and published in the 'Scientific Transactions' of the
Royal Dublin Society in 1880. Many of the objects listed in this work
were observed on more than one occasion, each individual observation being

Early Catalogues

separately recorded. The modern visual observer will recognise here a
familiar aspect of his own experience; namely, that due to a variety of
reasons, such as the condition of the telescope optics, atmospheric seeing
and transparency, the appearance of a particular object can vary greatly
from one occasion to another.

Lord Rosse's 'Leviathan' achieved its results despite two major
obstacles in the way of operating the huge instrument: these were its
mounting which restricted observations to within an hour or so of the
meridian - and the Irish climate. William Lassell, a wealthy Liverpool
brewer and amateur astronomer, sought to overcome such limitations by
constructing first a 24-inch, and then a 48-inch reflector, both of which
he transported to the island of Malta. During the years 1861 to 1865,
Lassell, together with his adept assistant, Albert Marth, used the 48-inch
to great effect, resulting in the discovery of some 600 new nebulae, most
of which have turned out to be faint galaxies. Lassell published his
'List of 600 Nebulae found at Malta...' in the 'Philosophical Transactions'
in 1864.

In this latter half of the nineteenth century the search for new nebulae
had to be extended to fainter and fainter limits and many new and skilled
observers entered this challenging field. Foremost among them were
Barnard, Bond, Burnham, Holden and Swift in America and Bigourdan, Lohse,
Schmidt, Schulz, Stephan, Tempel and Winnecke in Europe.

These observers reaped a rich harvest and it soon became apparent that
John Herschel's 'General Catalogue' needed a complete revision and
updating. This task was promoted by the Royal Astronomical Society in 1886
by commissioning J.L.E. Dreyer, formerly an assistant to Lord Rosse, to
compile all the then known nebulae and star clusters into one new
catalogue. Dreyer was responsive to the challenge and in 1888 he
submitted for publication what has turned out to be one of the most famous
astronomical catalogues ever to be produced.

The 'New General Catalogue' contained 7840 entries, and even with the
few duplications and other minor inaccuracies involved, it still remains a
popular reference work, especially among amateur astronomers. The NGC
numbers attached to each object are still universally employed as a
standard reference for the brighter deep-sky objects.

It has been estimated that about 85% of the NGC entries refer to objects
which are now recognised as galaxies, thus again revealing the dominance of
this class over all others. By this time one might have thought that
virtually all the visually observable nebulae had been discovered and
recorded, but in fact additional new discoveries were being made at an

Early Catalogues

even faster rate; so much so that in 1895, Dreyer was compelled to publish his first supplement to the NGC.

The first 'Index Catalogue', again published by the R.A.S., contained 1529 objects, almost all of which are galaxies. The major contributors to this catalogue were Bigourdan, Swift, Javelle and Burnham, but in addition to these visual observers we now, for the first time, find objects listed which had been discovered photographically, by Max Wolf of Heidelburg. This new technique was only the initial example of what would soon be the principal method of future discovery.

In 1908 Dreyer produced his 'Second Index Catalogue' which listed 3867 new objects, mostly discovered by means of the rapidly developing astro-camera. By 1908 then, the positions and brief descriptions of some 13,226 objects had been gathered together into the New General Catalogue and its two Index supplements, providing a reference of vital importance to this branch of observational astronomy.

The last significant catalogue of deep-sky objects based upon visual observation was that compiled by Guillaume Bigourdan during the years 1884 to 1909. This monumental survey of all the NGC objects was carried out with the 12-inch equatorial telescope at Paris observatory, and its outstanding merit lies in the meticulous accuracy of its position measurements. It was unfortunate for Bigourdan that his work was undertaken at a time when the astro-camera was already replacing the human eye for the observation of faint nebulae and no doubt because of this his catalogue was largely overlooked by other astronomers. Even so, the modern amateur deep-sky observer who is lucky enough to have access to Bigourdan's catalogue will find it a mine of valuable information for the identification of faint galaxies.

To obtain the maximum advantage, however, the amateur who wishes to make significant progress in this field will need to turn to more modern catalogues, i.e. those produced after 1950, as a result of studies made of the Palomar Observatory Sky Survey prints. It is through these more recent works that the amateur visual observer can, if he chooses, begin to reap the vast, unharvested regions of the visually undiscovered 'anonymous galaxies', whose numbers exceed all those alluded to previously in this chapter.

. . . .

3. MODERN CATALOGUES OF GALAXIES

With the completion and distribution of the prints of the Palomar Observatory Sky Survey in 1956, it soon became obvious to those researchers who had examined them that, because of the vast number of new unlisted galaxy images revealed, a new catalogue or catalogues were necessary. In the following years therefore, astronomers from different countries became involved in the difficult task of evaluating the prints, and from the derived information, publishing updated catalogues.

During the 25-year period following the publication of the Palomar survey, five major catalogues have been published based upon the studies of the prints and of these, three deal only with galaxies. It is essential that anyone interested in the visual study of anonymous galaxies have access to at least one of these catalogues and it is also imperative that any serious observer in this field have available the opportunity to examine the prints of the Sky Survey. This should not prove too difficult, as most universities having any sort of major physical science programme will have a copy in their library.

Each of these catalogues will be described in detail:

1. Morphological Catalogue of Galaxies by Prof. B.A. Vorontsov-Velyaminov, (4 volumes) 1962-68, Moscow State University, Moscow.

This outstanding work contains information on about 29,000 galaxies north of declination -33° and goes down to a photographic magnitude of 15.

This catalogue is divided into 10 columns, as follows:

Column 1: the number of the galaxy, based upon its order of R.A. in a given field. Some numbers have an asterisk indicating additional information is available concerning the object in the footnotes.

Column 2: the NGC or IC number if applicable.

Column 3: co-ordinates for the object, epoch 1950.

Column 4: the integral magnitude (m).

Column 5: the size of the galaxy's inner structure, measured in tenths of an arc minute (d).

Column 6: the overall size of the galaxy, also in tenths of an arc minute (D).

Modern Catalogues

Column 7: the surface brightness of the inner part of the galaxy, based upon a six point scale (Id).

Column 8: the surface brightness of the outer part of the galaxy, based upon a six point scale (ID).

Column 9: the inclination of the galaxy's major axis to the line of sight, based upon a five point numerical scale (i).

Column 10: a description of the appearance of each galaxy, based upon its visible image on the Palomar print, this description being provided by a series of lettered symbols.

This catalogue is generally accurate in the information and identities except that found in Column 4, but as noted by Vorontsov-Velyaminov, the magnitudes listed are strictly estimates subject to considerable error. When photometric magnitudes were available, they were included and so noted. Column 10, which describes the appearance of the galaxies, was obtained by examining the photographic images with a 20-power binocular magnifier, each galaxy being described from its central area out to its visual edge. The descriptions employed in this catalogue are achieved by using lettered symbols, and a detailed explanation of this system is provided in the introduction to Volume 1 of the catalogue, this explanation being translated into English.

2. Catalogue of Galaxies and Clusters of Galaxies by F. Zwicky et al., (6 volumes), California Institute of Technology, Pasadena, California.

This six volume work is probably the most accurate as regards to its information concerning the co-ordinates and photographic magnitudes of the galaxies it contains. It lists some 31,350 separate galaxies, and also provides information on 9,700 clusters of galaxies. The catalogue is divided into sections, each equivalent to an individual Palomar print (36 square degrees). Each section is accompanied by a chart on which every individual galaxy listed in the catalogue is noted, and every cluster of galaxies pertaining to the region is plotted. The individual galaxies are shown by symbols of brightness, while each cluster of galaxies is identified by a line showing the extent of the cluster, each cluster being numbered.

Directly beneath each chart the following information is provided: (i) Field Number, (ii) Survey Plate Number and (iii) a list of GC stars, where co-ordinates for epoch 1950 are given, plus photographic magnitudes.

Those sections dealing with clusters of galaxies list their approximate central co-ordinates (1950), their type or character, population, diameter

on the chart (in centimeters), a general reference to the distance, and
the number on the chart.

The section on individual galaxies lists their co-ordinates (1950), NGC
or IC number where applicable, photographic magnitude, and in some cases,
additional information such as radial velocities, types, and individual
peculiarities. The galaxies are complete to Mp 15.5, although galaxies to
Mp 15.7 are often included. This work can be relied on for the accuracy of
its co-ordinate positions and also its magnitude values, which are given to
tenths of a magnitude.

Although most of the galaxies listed are anonymous, as would be
expected, Zwicky did not assign any personal catalogue numbers to them,
preferring to apply the term 'anonymous', and leaving the accuracy of his
published co-ordinates to identify them. As one observer who has used
this catalogue's co-ordinates to identify many anonymous galaxies, I can
state that the published measurements, when applied to prints of the
Palomar Observatory Sky Survey, make the investigator's search for any
specific object an easy task. It has been my experience that when
differences of identity occur in the various catalogues, the CGCG turns
out to be correct. The major disappointment of the CGCG is that it does
not contain much descriptive information of the objects listed, but this
was not the purpose of the catalogue, and certainly in respect to its goals
it succeeds completely.

3. Uppsala General Catalogue of Galaxies by Peter Nilson, Uppsala, 1973.

Another work of excellence, containing a wealth of information on some
12,921 galaxies north of declination $-2^{o}.5$. Most of its information is
the result of studies of the Palomar prints, although some of its
information is derived from the CGCG.

The Uppsala General Catalogue is divided into 12 columns:

Column 1   - the galaxy's Uppsala Number

Column 2   - the co-ordinates for epoch 1950

Column 3(A) - the galaxy's MCG number
        (B) - the galaxy's NGC or IC number

Column 4(A) - number of the Palomar Survey field in which the object is
               best visible
        (B) - number of cluster in CGCG

Modern Catalogues

Column 5(A) - diameter as measured on the Blue Palomar print
        (B) - diameter as measured on the Red Palomar print

Column 6(A) - Position Angle of major axis
        (B) - estimated inclination to the line of sight of flattened
              galaxies on a scale of 1 - 7 (7 = edge-on)

Column 7   - Information Parameter, estimating the uncertainty in the
               classification, on a scale of 0 - 5 (0 = most uncertainty)

Column 8(A) - classification in Hubble system
        (B) - Luminosity Class according to van den Berg's system (only
              IV, IV-V and V)

Column 9(A) - classification according to de Vaucouleur's revised Hubble
               system
        (B) - classification according to Holmberg's revised Hubble
              system

Column 10   - apparent Mp from CGCG or, if fainter than 15.7, estimated
               from blue prints

Column 11(A) - Radial Velocity referred to the Sun
        (B) - Radial Velocity corrected for Solar motion

Column 12   - reference to the notes section, or other published
               catalogues

From this, the reader will immediately realise that this catalogue
contains almost all the information the observer might require in order to
search for and observe any galaxy which might be of interest. Certainly
for the visual observer it provides a great amount of follow-up information,
but it is not, however, completely free from the occasional error, especially
in correct identification. For the observer to be completely certain, it
is better if he has additional sources available in order to check out any
dubious identifications. Admittedly the identity errors may be very few
but as always, it is best to apply all available information when possible.

The Uppsala catalogue has many features which make it attractive to use;
foremost is the fact that all the information is contained in a single
volume, certainly an advantage when making observations at the telescope.
Secondly, as the co-ordinates and the Mp's are derived from the CGCG, any
observer, especially one using setting circles, will have no difficulty in
obtaining the correct field for any object. Also, the information about

14

Modern Catalogues

size, type and angle of major axis will help prepare the observer as to
what to look for in the field of view. Another asset of this catalogue
is the greatly detailed 'Notes' section which is to be found between pages
371 and 436.

The UGC is worth owning for the 'Notes' section alone as it provides a
wealth of information found in no other deep-sky catalogue. Not only are
particular features of galaxies covered, but references to many closely
associated objects are described. It is this catalogue that I use at
Westmont for my telescope work and I can highly recommend it. A further
feature of this catalogue which might prove attractive to observers is the
Precession Tables found on pages 438 - 444. These tables enable the
observer to change the co-ordinates of any galaxy from the 1950 epoch to
2000 epoch.

4. The Revised New General Catalogue of Non-stellar Astronomical Objects
by J.W. Sulentic and W.G. Tifft, Univ. of Arizona Press, 1973.

This catalogue, as the name implies, is an updated version of the
original NGC published in 1888. The original NGC was entirely based upon
information derived from visual observation of 7,840 objects, and this
revised catalogue re-examines those same objects, evaluating their
appearances as visible on the Palomar Observatory Sky Survey prints plus
some additional prints provided by several southern hemisphere
observatories. Of special interest is the comparison of descriptions
provided by the original visual observers and those obtained from
examination of the photographic images. It is significant that in many
cases, features in the brighter objects are often visually apparent in
moderately large aperture telescopes, but are lost on the long exposure
prints of the survey.

The RNGC is divided into 10 columns:

Column 1 - the RNGC number, which is the same as the original number

Column 2 - the type of object, indicated by numbers (1 - 10)

Column 3 - co-ordinates for epoch 1975 (generally accurate to 0.1 and 1
            minute of arc)

Column 4 - galactic longitude and latitude of the object

Column 5 - position of object on Palomar print (being measured in mm from
            the lower left hand corner of the relevant print)

Column 6 - photographic magnitude (rounded to nearest 0.5 Mp)

Modern Catalogues

Column 7 - Source of magnitude. A numerical code system is used to
indicate the following authorities:

1: de Vaucouleurs	5: Collinder
2: Zwicky	6: Arp
3: Vorontsov-Velyaminov	7: Vorontsov-Velyaminov (catalogue of integrated Mp of planetary nebulae)
4: Lindsay	8: Bok & van den Bergh

Column 8 - visual appearance recorded in the original NGC

Column 9 - description of object based upon its photographic image on the
relevant Sky Survey print

Column 10 - cross references to other catalogues, etc.

One may well enquire "what has this catalogue to do with anonymous
galaxies?" The answer lies in the fact that the RNGC does include
references to many of the anonymous galaxies closely associated with NGC
objects. Often, the associated anonymous object is assigned an affixed
letter, A, B, C etc., so that one finds for example NGC 1316 plus NGC 1316A,
NGC 1316B and NGC 1316C, these last three being associated anonymous
galaxies. In addition, column 10 often has references to the notes
sections 8 and 9, found following page 365, and here one often finds
reference to nearby anonymous galaxies. Notes Section 9 is quite limited,
being contained within only 1½ pages but Notes Section 8 consists of 12
pages, and as a result of the computer age, it lists many associated
galaxies in addition to information about the predominant NGC galaxy.

5. A Master List of Non-stellar Optical Astronomical Objects by R.S. Dixon
and G. Sonneborn, Ohio State Univ. Press, 1980.

This catalogue is a compendium of all the previously published
catalogues based upon examination of the Palomar prints. It is a triumph
of the computer age but suffers from an over abundance of unconnected
information. Its proposed purpose, according to its authors, is to be a
collection of all the relevant information available in the previously
published works. It is possible that this purpose was achieved, but the
information is so scattered and unconnected as to make it almost worthless.
As an example, one-line references to the same galaxy may appear 16 pages
apart so that the investigator becomes exhausted in trying to figure out
just what information concerning one object is available in this catalogue.
Likewise, since the publication of this catalogue, the same authors, in
conjunction with this work, have produced a series of overlay grids which
are to be used when examining prints of the Palomar Observatory Sky Survey.
Here again, in an effort to provide too much information, I feel the

Modern Catalogues

grids only serve to confuse, and personally I feel much more confident
with the uncluttered overlay grids provided with the original Palomar
prints.

I am certain that this catalogue in many respects is very accurate, but
it is a most difficult catalogue to use, and I would not feel confident in
recommending it to those who would wish to become involved in anonymous
galaxy study.

. . . .

Now a personal assessment of the values of these catalogues to a
beginner in the field of anonymous galaxies study. My first recommendation
would be that you acquire and use the RNGC. Why this catalogue? Well,
because all the anonymous galaxies it lists are located in the same field
of view as an NGC galaxy so that if you cannot see the one dominant NGC
object, then you will certainly not see the anonymous object. By using
the RNGC you will also have a reference point from which to attempt the
anonymous object. Beyond this, any of the other catalogues will suffice.
Remember, the more reference information you subject your own observations
to, the greater the probability of accuracy, and this, in the final
analysis, is what each of us wishes to achieve. To supplement the RNGC, I
would select the UGC, as I feel it provides the most pertinent information
required by the visual observer of anonymous galaxies.

. . . .

4. MODERN ATLASES AND CHARTS

In this chapter the reader will find a brief description of some atlases and charts available to the amateur astronomer. All of the works listed have been used by the writer (RJM) and because of this, a brief summary of the usefulness of each will follow its description. However, the reader must decide for himself which will best compliment his observing programme. For the purpose of this chapter, all charts and atlases will be compared as to their relative scale. To do this, each one was measured at 0 hours/0 degrees, travelling north.

1. Norton's Star Atlas and Reference Handbook (Epoch 1950), by Arthur P. Norton & J. Gall Inglis.

Norton's Star Atlas and Reference Handbook contains a set of eight star charts at the back of the book. Each chart measures approximately 17 inches by 11 inches (42½ cm x 28 cm) and shows stars down to magnitude 6.35. The scale of these charts are such that one inch equals approximately eight degrees. Some of the brighter or more popular deep-sky objects are shown on the charts, which cover the entire sky.

These charts are useful for locating the general area of the sky desired, and would be useful to the novice or one using a small telescope or a pair of binoculars. I cannot however, recommend these small scale charts to the serious observer, especially one attempting to observe anonymous galaxies.

2. Atlas of the Heavens (Atlas Coeli)(Epoch 1950), by Antonin Becvar.

Also known as the Skalnate Pleso Atlas, this work shows stars down to visual magnitude 7.75, some 32,571 altogether. This atlas can be found in three editions: (i) white stars on a black background, (ii) black stars on a white background, and (iii) a colour edition which has a larger scale than the first two. There are a total of sixteen charts covering the entire sky. Each chart (colour edition) measures 23 inches by 16 inches (58 cm x 40 cm), border to border. The scale is such that one inch equals 3.4 degrees. A large number of deep-sky objects are shown on this atlas, 293 open star clusters, 100 globular clusters, 144 planetary nebulae, 245 bright diffuse nebulae, 1210 extra-galactic nebulae and a good number of dark nebulae. All of the brighter or well-known deep-sky objects are labelled with the appropriate NGC/IC or other number. The dark nebulae, however, are not labelled. A transparent grid overlay is provided with the colour edition only. A companion 'Atlas of the Heavens - II: Catalogue', containing information on all of the objects shown in the atlas, is obtainable separately.

This atlas/catalogue combination presents the observer with a great deal

Modern Atlases and Charts

of information concerning celestial objects. The colour edition of the atlas is to be preferred over the two black & white editions - not only because of the grid overlay which accompanies it, but also because of the larger scale. These charts are useful for finding the general vicinity of any deep-sky object sought, including any objects one may plot on this atlas. Often, a faint star shown on this atlas will be in the general area of a deep-sky object (or anonymous galaxy) one is seeking. This 'faint' star can then be used as a reference point for locating the object in question. I recommend this atlas for the serious observer.

3. Sky Atlas 2000.0 (Epoch 2000), by Wil Tirion.

The 'Sky Atlas 2000.0' comes in three editions, black stars on white, white stars on black and a colour edition, in the same way as the 'Atlas of the Heavens'. This atlas, however, is set for epoch 2000 and shows stars down to magnitude 8.0, 45,000 being plotted. The large number of deep-sky objects shown is similar to the 'Atlas of the Heavens', except that dark nebulae are not generally shown. All of the deep-sky objects listed in the Sky Atlas are labelled regardless of brightness or size. The colour edition consists of 26 charts, each measuring $20\frac{1}{2}$ x $15\frac{1}{2}$ inches (51 cm x 39 cm), border to border. The scale of the colour edition, which is larger than either of the black & white editions, is such that one inch equals $3\frac{1}{3}$ degrees. A transparent grid overlay accompanies the colour edition. A catalogue in two volumes is available, giving data for all of the objects shown on the atlas.

This work can be considered as an updated version of the 'Atlas of the Heavens'. The fact that all deep-sky objects are labelled and that fainter stars are shown is an added plus, however, the omission of dark nebulae may be objected to by some. This atlas can also be recommended to all serious observers.

4. Smithsonian Astrophysical Observatory Star Atlas of Reference Stars and Non-stellar Objects, by the staff of the S.A.O.

The 'Smithsonian Astrophysical Observatory Atlas' (SAO) is composed of 152 loose charts, each one measuring 11 x 14 inches (20 cm x 35 cm) in size, border to border. Here we find some 260,000 stars of magnitude 9.0 or brighter, although some stars down to magnitude 11 are shown. Measurements show that a scale ratio is such that one inch equals three degrees. Besides showing the relative positions of the stars, this atlas includes all of the NGC and IC objects, even those that are non-existent. Also included are those objects listed in Shapley's 'Star Clusters', Shapley & Ames' 'A Survey of the External Galaxies brighter than the 13th Magnitude' and Vorontsov-Velyaminov's 'Catalogue of Planetary Nebulae'. A four volume set, called the SAO Star Catalogue, and a book listing the

Modern Atlases and Charts

non-stellar objects in the SAO, compliment the SAO Atlas. The scale of
the SAO Atlas is closely compatible with either the 'Atlas of the Heavens'
or the 'Sky Atlas 2000.0'. It is a simple matter to transpose from one
atlas to another. The major fault of the SAO is that it indicates deep-
sky objects whether they exist or not. Several galaxies may be shown in a
small area where in fact only one or two exist - this could be confusing
to a novice. The user of this atlas should consult a reference book on
the type of deep-sky object he wishes to observe; one cannot rely solely
on this atlas. Even so, I can still recommend it to serious observers.

5. A.A.V.S.O. Variable Star Atlas (Epoch 1950), by Charles E. Scovil.

This atlas shows stars down to visual magnitude 9.5. It is made up of
a set of 178 loose, boxed charts, each one measuring 14 x 12 inches (35 cm
x 30 cm) in size, border to border. The scale is such that one inch equals
$1\frac{3}{4}$ degrees, making it considerably larger than the SAO (which was in fact
used as a reference for the AAVSO atlas). Many deep-sky objects are shown,
including all of the Messier objects, all galaxies listed in the Shapley-
Ames catalogue, selected bright open star clusters, globular clusters,
diffuse and planetary nebulae which are included in the SAO list of non-
stellar objects. Generally, the number of deep-sky objects shown on this
atlas is less than the number shown on the SAO.

Because of the large scale of this atlas it is a simple matter to plot
in any object (such as an anonymous galaxy) desired. The one disadvantage
is the absence of a transparent grid overlay, a problem which could be
overcome by making one's own. This is an excellent atlas and I can
thoroughly recommend it to serious observers.

6. Stern Atlas (Falkauer Atlas) (Epoch 1950), by Hans Vehrenberg.

This atlas consists of 303 photographic prints, showing stars down to
the 13th photographic magnitude. This is accomplished for the sky down to
Declination -26°. Two editions are available, black stars on a white
background and white stars on a black background. Each print, not
including the border, measures 7 x 7 inches (18 cm x 18 cm) in size, while
the entire loose print measures 12 x $18\frac{1}{4}$ inches (30 cm x 21 cm) across.
The scale is such that one inch equals nearly $1\frac{3}{4}$ degrees (15mm = 1 degree).
These prints were taken with a 71mm aperture lens of 210mm focal length
and show some 10 x 10 degrees of sky. A set of ten transparent grid
overlays accompanies these prints.

I find the scale of these prints to be a bit small for plotting in my
own deep-sky objects and generally they appear to be too crowded with
stars. Although these prints may have limited use for the observer, I

Modern Atlases and Charts

do not feel able to recommend them to the serious observer in search of anonymous galaxies.

7. Atlas Stellarum (Epoch 1950), by Hans Vehrenberg.

This atlas is a bound (ring binder) set of 450 photographic prints, covering the sky from pole to pole. Black stars are shown on a white background, with a limiting photographic magnitude of about 14.0. The actual print size measures 13 x 13 inches (33 cm. x 33 cm.) in size, while the entire plate size, border to border, is 15 x 14¼ inches (38 cm. x 36 cm.) in size. Each print covers an area of sky 10 degrees x 10 degrees, the scale being such that 1-inch equals 7/8 of a degree (1 mm = 2 arcmin.). These prints were made with a 120 mm aperture lens of 540 mm focal length. Ten transparent grid overlays come with this atlas.

Because of the larger scale of this atlas, it is better suited for the visual deep-sky observer than is the 'Stern Atlas'. Many of the brighter deep-sky objects can be found. Galaxies, however, do not fare as well as the other types of object, unless they are bright. The scale is large enough for one to plot one's own deep-sky objects (anonymous galaxies) and this will give the observer a general idea of just what stars will be in the area of the object sought. This atlas I can recommend to the serious observer.

8. True Visual Magnitude Photographic Star Atlas (Epoch 1950), by C. Papadopoulos (Vol. 1 & 2) and C. Papadopoulos & C. Scovil (Vol. 3).

This atlas consists of a total of 456 loose (boxed) photographic prints, in three volumes which cover the entire sky. Each print gives us an 11 degree x 11 degree field and shows black stars on a white background. The prints themselves are 13 x 13 inches (33 cm. x 33 cm.) in size, while the total print size, border to border, is 16 x 15½ inches (40 cm. x 39 cm.). The scale of these charts was measured where 1-inch equals 5/6 of a degree. These prints are neither red nor blue sensitive, but rather sensitive to the visual spectrum. In other words, these prints show the stars as they would appear visually through a telescope. The limiting magnitude is given as 13.5. A set of transparent grid overlays is supplied.

These prints are unusual in that they show the stars as they appear to the eye as seen through a telescope. The usual red or blue sensitive prints favour either red or blue stars, but this 'visual' atlas favours neither. This is an added plus for the visual observer. The stellar images are surprisingly small and sharp. The scale is large enough to permit one to plot in deep-sky objects, such as anonymous galaxies. As with the photographic atlases listed above, galaxies (unless bright) do

Modern Atlases and Charts

not fare well. Even so, this is an excellent atlas for the serious
observer.

9. Palomar Observatory Sky Survey (Epoch 1950), by National Geographic
Society.

The Palomar Observatory Sky Survey (P.O.S.S.) contains a total of 879
loose bound red sensitive and blue sensitive prints. These prints, taken
with the 48-inch (1.2 m.) Schmidt telescope, cover the sky down to -27°.
The red prints have a limiting magnitude of 20.0, while the blue prints
go down to magnitude 21.1. Each print measures $13\frac{1}{2}$ x $13\frac{1}{2}$ inches (34 cm.
x 34 cm.) in size while the total size, including borders, measures
17 x 14 inches ($42\frac{1}{2}$ cm. x 35 cm.). The position of the print centre
(epoch 1950) is shown on the northeast corner of each print. The scale
is such that one inch equals almost $\frac{1}{2}$ of a degree. A set of transparent
grid overlays can be purchased separately.

These prints make excellent finder charts for the observer seeking
faint galaxies as galaxies show up pretty well on this atlas. It may not
be necessary to plot in an anonymous galaxy; it is very likely that it
can be identified on the prints. Generally the blue sensitive prints
show galaxies better but this is not always the case. These are superior
to any of the other photographic prints discussed above. I recommend
the use of these to all serious observers.

. . . .

5. VISUAL OBSERVATION

Most of the readers of this volume of the 'Handbook', we imagine, are astronomical observers who have already graduated in observational technique and have acquired considerable skill in the finer aspects of their craft. To deal with elementary details of observing method would therefore be superfluous, and in the following pages only the special requirements of observing anonymous galaxies will be discussed. In general, however, it need only be emphasised that in this somewhat more advanced field of amateur astronomy, every stage in the process needs to be finely tuned to as near perfection as possible. Whatever telescope is used, it, and its accessories, need to be in peak condition; the location should be chosen with the object of avoiding light-polluted skies; the observer's visual acuity should be well trained and - above all - the motivation to succeed should be of the highest. Skill, painstaking attention to detail and determination will always produce results.

Telescope Aperture and Mounting.

Even though large-aperture telescopes are to be preferred when observing anonymous galaxies, amateurs having access to telescopes as small as 12-inch (30.5 cm.) aperture can still be encouraged to seek out these faint galaxies. As with any type of deep-sky object, we find a considerable number of brighter examples, and some of these, in fact, may even be seen in instruments no larger than 10-inch (25.4 cm.) aperture. Whatever the light-gathering capacity of the telescope employed, it should be remembered that the number of anonymous galaxies present in almost any chosen field of view is truly enormous, and while most of these may not be seen, the number of positive observations will, in all probability, be high.

When discussing the types of telescope mountings available for amateur use, we are entering the area of personal preference and even prejudice. It suffices to say that by the time the observer is contemplating the search for anonymous galaxies, he should be capable of handling his telescope, whatever mounting it has, with expert ease. While the equatorially-mounted telescope, accurately aligned, and fitted with a reliable drive, has many advantages, such a set-up is not an absolute necessity. Many of the larger instruments in use nowadays are of an alt-azimuth or Dobsonian type, and while the application of a computer controlled tracking system would be quite feasible for the expert handyman, this, too, could be looked upon as a luxury. A simple form of 'computer-controlled' setting for alt-azimuth mounted telescopes is given in Appendix 2.

Visual Observation

Whatever type of mounting is used it is absolutely vital that the controls are easy to operate, and the motions perfectly smooth in both axes. One must remember that it may be necessary to examine each field of view for a considerable time - perhaps 30 minutes or more - in order to make a positive identification, and with a fairly high magnification in use, the area will have to be kept in view with smooth precision.

Accessories.

Today's astro-market presents the amateur with an almost endless variety of telescope accessories but there are only a few which have any special application to the observation of anonymous galaxies. The choice of eyepiece is of course a very important matter, although it should be considered, not merely as an accessory, but as part of the essential optical train of the telescope itself. Only experience will show what type of eyepiece gives the best performance in combination with the particular O.G. or mirror/flat arrangement in the rest of the system. Many observers find that high-quality orthoscopic oculars perform well in most instruments, while one of the present authors (MJT) has a preference for the Plossll eyepiece when used in fairly short focus reflectors. If one's eyepieces give good definition out to the edge of the visible field, together with the impression of a good dark background to the whole field, all is well.

Whatever type of eyepiece is used it will be necessary for anonymous galaxy observation to have at least three stages of magnification: a low power for locating the proper field required; a medium power for the first examination in detail and, finally, a high power to magnify the smaller images to establish whether they are nebulous or not. In general, three oculars in the ranges 32mm - 19mm (LP), 18mm - 10mm (MP), and 10mm or less (HP) should prove sufficient.

The next most important accessory is the finderscope: too often those supplied with commercial telescopes are too small for serious work. This is especially so when trying to locate the 'immediate area' of the sky where an anonymous galaxy lies. In order to transfer one's orientation from the star chart to the sky itself one needs a good finderscope of at least 8x50 or 10x40 specification. One other common fault with such instruments is mis-alignment, and this cannot be tolerated when attempting to observe anonymous galaxies. The alignment of the finderscope with the optical axis of the main telescope must be checked frequently and with care.

Another useful accessory (which most observers possess, but which is often under-employed) is a good pair of binoculars. Often there will be

Visual Observation

a faint star, of 6th to 8th magnitude, within the field of view of the anonymous galaxy one is searching for. Locating the star visually will be facilitated by the use of binoculars, and this will make its identification in the finderscope much easier.

Finally, a most useful luxury is an adjustable observing chair. For extended observing, especially when engaged in drawing at the telescope, a comfortable seat is a great asset. A detailed design, for construction by the home handyman, was provided by Colin Pither in Webb Society Quarterly Journal No. 35 (January 1979).

Observing Sites.

On the location of an observing site one thing can be stated at the outset: the 'ideal' site does not exist! If it is ideally dark, it is certain to be so remote as to be almost inaccessible, and for the amateur astronomer who probably has to live within commuting distance of a large conurbation some compromise has to be sought. For observing anonymous galaxies one needs a fairly large telescope, and if one's 'home' site is light-polluted, it may be difficult to make the instrument readily transportable.

Failing this, it may be possible to rent a small outbuilding from a friendly farmer or smallholder for use as an observatory: then, at least, one's travelling may be relatively unencumbered. Another possibility is to search out an existing observatory in a good location where use of the existing facilities can be obtained. There are many excellent large telescopes in various places which are little used – and even neglected: their owners or controlling bodies will often prove to be most co-operative, especially if presented with a serious observing programme.

Whatever the 'practical' steps that are taken, it should be emphasised that the choice of location is at least as important as the choice of the telescope itself. This holds especially true for the observation of anonymous galaxies. In considering the value of any potential observing site, the darkness of the sky should be carefully assessed on a number of occasions. One easy method involves only one's eyes. Using direct vision, find and identify the faintest naked-eye star visible at or near the zenith. The magnitude of this star can then be compared with that of the faintest stars seen in similar conditions at other localities. As a guide one could dismiss any site where the faintest star seen was brighter than magnitude 3.5; from mag. 3.6 – 4.5 can be rated as poor; from mag. 4.6 – 5.5 might be considered acceptable, while mag. 5.6 or fainter would be excellent.

So far we have considered only the transparency of the night sky, and

Visual Observation

while this is very important, the steadiness of the atmosphere, or
'seeing', must also be taken into consideration, and this, too, may vary
considerably from site to site. Many observers, in fact, consider the
seeing to be an even more important factor than transparency. To assess
the quality of the seeing it will be necessary to take a portable
telescope to the site on a number of occasions when the skies are clear,
but with different directions of wind and atmospheric stability. Using a
fairly high power ocular, a familiar deep-sky object or a planet should
be viewed for an extended period: any evidence of 'boiling' or wavering
of the image persisting for any length of time will indicate poor seeing
at the site.

Finally, before deciding on a site, one should be aware of any 'hidden'
snags which may arise. It may be quite free from general and permanent
light-pollution, but the presence of a nearby road may mean that the
lights of passing motorists may impinge upon the site from time to time.
It may be possible to reduce the effect of this by the erection of
screens, providing that the interference is not too frequent or too
severe.

Another hazard is the presence of nearby buildings, especially if they
are of concrete construction: they will continue to radiate heat long
after the sun has set, and if in the observer's line of sight, will play
havoc with the seeing.

Needless to say, the search for anonymous galaxies is not likely to be
profitable with any significant amount of moonlight present, or in any
period of astronomical twilight. And for the detection of the most
difficult objects, the best results can be obtained when the object in
question is within, say, one hour of the local meridian.

Observing Techniques.

Searching for faint anonymous galaxies can no longer be considered
out of the realm of amateur astronomers. In fact, the art of observing
anonymous galaxies is fast becoming an ever increasing addition to the
observing programmes of many serious amateurs. This can be seen as a
logical sequence in view of the fact that the number of galaxies visible
through amateur sized telescopes exceeds the combined total of all other
types of deep-sky objects (stars excluded). This recent rise in
popularity of anonymous galaxies can be attributed to two major events.
The first is the number of large-aperture instruments in the hands of
amateurs today, the second is the availability of reference data on
anonymous galaxies provided for the amateur astronomer.

One problem that the observer of anonymous galaxies faces is that of

Visual Observation

proper identification of the correct field of view. The galaxy itself
may require averted vision to see; that is, if it can be seen at all! It
is not uncommon to have the correct field of view, i.e., the one
containing the anonymous galaxy, but to see nothing but stars because the
galaxy may be too faint to be seen visually. It will be obvious, even to
the casual observer, that this is more difficult than identifying the
field of a bright object, such as the planetary nebula M.57. In this
case the correct field is identified by locating the planetary nebula,
and not by the field stars themselves. This is not the case, however,
with anonymous galaxies which themselves may be 'invisible' in the field.
To confuse this matter further, there may be two or more galaxies in the
field, not all of which may be visible. Identification now becomes
somewhat more difficult, but not impossible. There are times when a
'bright' NGC or IC deep-sky object will be seen in the same field as an
anonymous galaxy. We can then use this brighter object as our reference
point, making identification of our anonymous galaxy less difficult. As
complex as all of this seems, the amateur armed with the proper equipment
can successfully locate and identify many anonymous galaxies.

The following account is a step-by-step procedure for locating these
faint galaxies. For an example we will use the anonymous galaxy known
as ZWG 539.012. This is associated with the NGC 910 galaxy group, also
listed as No. 347 in Abell's list of clusters of galaxies. Abell 347 is
not a difficult group of galaxies to locate and is described in the
'Webb Society Deep-Sky Observer's Handbook: Volume 5' (Clusters of
Galaxies), pp. 119-123. The first step is to find the co-ordinates and
photographic magnitude of ZWG 539.012. This information can be found in
the set of books titled 'A Catalogue of Galaxies and Clusters of Galaxies'
by Fritz Zwicky (Vols. 1-6). From this reference work we learn that the
important statistics are: R.A. 02h. 22.0m., Dec. +41°.38 (1950), Mp 14.9.
This information can also be found in other reference works pertaining to
faint galaxies. One important fact to remember, however, is that each
reference names and numbers these faint galaxies according to its own
system. It is obvious from this that our anonymous galaxy ZWG 539.012
will have a different name and number, depending on which reference book
you use.

While looking at our reference book, you will notice that several
other brighter galaxies are close to ZWG 539.012. Almost all of these
galaxies have a New General Catalogue number and therefore should be
easier to see visually than our anonymous galaxy. These nearby NGC
objects include: 898, 906, 909, 910, 911, 912, 914 and 923. Since we
have the co-ordinates for ZWG 539.012, we can use these to plot our
galaxy on a star atlas, such as the Atlas Coeli or Sky Atlas 2000.0.
Another method would be to use one set of co-ordinates to plot the entire

Visual Observation

Fig. 1. Galaxies in the Cluster Abell 347, including ZWG 539.012
(underlined).

Position a 1950 δ	NGC IC*	m_p	V_s km/sec	Remarks
h m o '				
2 19.8 + 42 47		15.2		
2 20.0 + 41 09		14.1		peculiar
2 20.0 + 42 46		15.0		double system
2 20.2 + 41 44	898	13.8		
2 20.8 + 41 59		15.7		
2 20.9 + 41 46		14.8		
2 21.4 + 40 39		15.1		
2 21.6 + 41 28		15.7		diffuse
2 21.6 + 41 48		15.7		
2 21.6 + 42 24		14.3		compact
2 21.7 + 43 06		15.6		compact
2 22.0 + 41 38		14.9		
2 22.0 + 45 15		15.5		
2 22.1 + 41 52	906	14.4		
2 22.2 + 41 30		15.7		compact
2 22.2 + 41 49	909	14.5		
2 22.3 + 41 36	910	14.5		star superposed
2 22.3 + 41 41		15.7		compact
2 22.6 + 40 55		15.5		
2 22.6 + 41 33	912	15.0		very compact
2 22.6 + 41 45	911	14.0		
2 22.6 + 43 23		15.6		
2 22.9 + 41 55	914	13.9		
2 23.6 + 41 37		15.0		
2 23.7 + 41 28		15.3		
2 23.7 + 41 48		15.7		
2 23.8 + 42 35		15.7		
2 24.2 + 40 50		15.2		very compact
2 24.3 + 41 42		15.7		
2 24.4 + 41 45	923	14.4		
2 24.4 + 41 47		15.0		
2 26.3 + 42 02	937	15.0		
2 27.3 + 41 14		15.7		compact
2 27.5 + 42 01	946	14.5		compact
2 28.0 + 43 07		15.7		
2 28.1 + 40 10		14.7		
2 28.1 + 43 15		15.0		
2 28.3 + 40 02		15.7		very compact
2 28.4 + 41 20		15.6		
2 29.0 + 43 14		15.4		
2 29.2 + 41 59		14.6		

(From 'Catalogue of Galaxies and Clusters of Galaxies', F. Zwicky)

Visual Observation

group of galaxies, in this case Abell 347. Usually the co-ordinates for
the brightest member of the cluster (NGC 910) would be used to represent
the entire group of galaxies. A small cross (+) can be used to designate
the object plotted, whether it be a lone galaxy or the entire cluster of
galaxies. Be certain to label your 'new' object so that you know just
what these newly plotted symbols represent. This is especially important
when, after years of plotting your own objects, you wind up with
hundreds of symbols on your star atlas. Without having each one labelled
you are apt to become confused as to what they represent.

Now that we have our galaxy group (or lone galaxy) plotted on our star
atlas, we make a note of its position among the stars. Almost at once it
will be noted that the bright galaxy NGC 891 lies less than 2/3 of a
degree northwest from Abell 347. This easy-to-locate bright galaxy can be
used as a reference point for locating Abell 347, which in turn can be
used to locate our anonymous galaxy ZWG 539.012.

Using our atlas, with the newly plotted galaxy group, we should be
able to locate its immediate area in the sky. When we look through the
telescope however, we will see much more detail than is shown on our small
scale atlas. We will now require a larger scale atlas, showing stars
down to magnitude 9 or fainter. Two star atlases which can be utilised
are the Smithsonian Astrophysical Observatory (SAO) Star Atlas or the
AAVSO Star Atlas. One set of prints that make excellent finder charts is
the Palomar Observatory Sky Survey (P.O.S.S.), but these are not always
available to the amateur. Once you have chosen your large scale atlas,
you may need to plot the galaxies individually on this atlas. Some
atlases, such as the SAO, usually lists NGC/IC objects, but you will need
to plot the anonymous galaxies. Atlases vary as to what deep-sky objects
they list but you can almost always count on having to add the anonymous
galaxies. Once this is done, you will have a map of the area that can be
used as a guide when viewing through the eyepiece. Certain recognizable
star patterns or groups of stars can usually be identified, both on this
chart and through the eyepiece. When observing any group of galaxies,
pay particular attention to the positions of the galaxies relative to
each other, as this will aid in identification. The field-of-view
drawings in this book are excellent for comparing to your own view as seen
through your telescope, or to be compared with your own field drawings.

Now that we have all of the galaxies, including our anonymous galaxy,
plotted on both our small and large scale atlases, we are ready to begin
observing. I first noticed the galaxy ZWG 539.012 while using a 13-inch
(33 cm.) telescope under clear skies. This is most likely near the
minimum aperture required to see this faint galaxy, depending on sky
conditions.

Visual Observation

Figure 2.   Diagram of the general area of the Abell 347 cluster of
            galaxies.

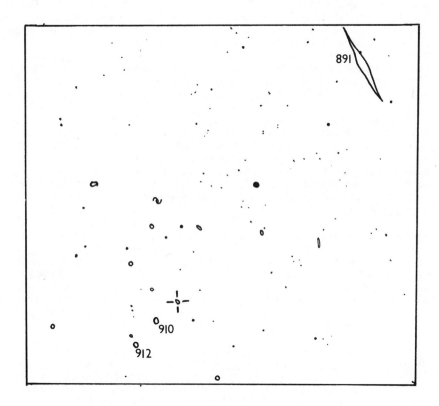

Visual Observation

In order to locate this anonymous galaxy, we are going to proceed from one reference point to another, until it is found. Our first reference point is the bright galaxy NGC 891. One easy method for locating this galaxy is to place the bright star γ Andromedae (mag. 2.28) in the centre of your low power field. Let the sky drift for 19.2 minutes and NGC 891 will appear in your field. Once you have found NGC 891, move your field approximately 2/3 of a degree to the southeast. On both Atlas Coeli and Sky Atlas 2000.0 you will notice a star plotted between NGC 891 and where we plotted Abell 347. Using a medium power ocular to scan this area to the southeast of NGC 891 the Abell cluster of galaxies should be found. Once you have looked over this area using the medium power ocular, switch to a high power ocular to pick up any faint galaxies missed. If you have difficulty locating Abell 347, use your large scale chart to 'star hop' from NGC 891 to the immediate area of the galaxy group.

The number of faint galaxies seen in the Abell 347 area may be somewhat confusing at first; because of this, drawings should be made so that they can be checked with photos or other drawings at a later time. The North point should be shown on your drawings. This is not difficult to ascertain while observing. Place an object (star or galaxy) near the centre of your field and let it drift until it reaches the edge of the field. This point at the edge of your field will be the eastern edge. The edge directly opposite will, of course, be the western edge. The north and south points will be at right angles to the line joining the eastern and western points. To confirm which is the north point take your eye away from the eyepiece and locate Polaris (in the northern hemisphere) with the naked eye. Note its position and return to the eyepiece. Push the telescope slightly in the direction of Polaris while looking through the eyepiece and note the direction of travel of the field. This will identify the north point of the field and obviously, the opposite point will be south. It is very important to know these points in your field, especially when you have more than one unknown object present.

It is not always possible to identify positively the unknown objects in your field <u>at the time of observation</u>; because of this a drawing or verbal description, written or tape-recorded, describing one object relative to another can help with identification at a later date. One example of a verbal description might be similar to the following: "Galaxy A is round, brighter than but smaller than Galaxy B, which itself is located a short distance south following Galaxy A. Galaxy C, found just north preceding Galaxy A, is also round but is smaller and fainter than either Galaxy A or Galaxy B. Galaxy B is definitely extended in shape". This description not only compares the three galaxies but also gives their positions in relation to each other. This will help when you are trying to identify the three galaxies as seen in your field. In

Visual Observation

Figure 3. Field drawing showing the anonymous galaxy ZWG 539.012.

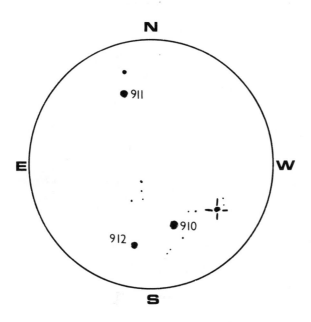

Observer: Ronald J. Morales
Instrument: 13.1-inch (33 cm.), f/4.5 reflector.
Ocular: 10.2 mm.

Visual Observation

the above example, south following (S.f.) refers to southeast while north preceding (N.p.) refers to northwest.

While observing Abell 347 try to identify NGC 910, which may appear as the brightest member of this group, followed closely in visual brightness by NGC 911. Identifying NGC 910 is important because we will use this galaxy as our next reference point for locating ZWG 539.012. Once you have located NGC 910 you should notice NGC 912 a little distance to the southeast (S.f.). Refer to your large scale chart. These two galaxies should fit easily into your medium power field. Take notice of the distance from NGC 910 to NGC 912. Starting from NGC 912, take a line through NGC 910 to a point which is the same distance from NGC 910 as NGC 910 is from NGC 912. This is the immediate area where ZWG 539.012 can be found. If you fail to find it, scan the area with a higher power ocular.

The amateur who takes the time to preplan his or her observing will reap benefits worth many times the effort. Preplanning is especially important when searching for any faint object. There is little doubt that an amateur with a large aperture instrument will come across faint anonymous galaxies while sweeping the area. But here, identification becomes extremely difficult, unless of course a bright NGC or IC object happens to be in the same field. Having found a faint object but not being able to identify it or find it again is not only unscientific but also unsatisfying. By preplanning particular objects, as has already been described, we have the satisfaction of making a positive identification of an object plus the knowledge that we can find it again. There will be times when the galaxy in question cannot be seen visually. In cases such as this, it is extremely important that the observer have the exact field, so that you are positive you are looking at the exact spot where the galaxy is located. Then, and only then, can you be certain that this galaxy was not seen. In many respects a negative observation is just as important as a positive one.

Identification and Confirmation.

An observer can expect to spend some time preplanning his or her night's observing, especially if seeking anonymous galaxies. A certain amount of time will also be spent in checking the observations after the observing period. This, of course, can be carried out at a later date, as time permits. Confirming the anonymous galaxies seen is not always easy and requires that the observer search through some galaxy catalogues and photographs.

If the anonymous galaxy seen is the only one in your field of view,

Visual Observation

then identification is not usually difficult. Part of preplanning
involves picking out just which anonymous galaxies we plan to observe.
It is at this time that we will find the co-ordinates of the galaxy in
question; this can be found in any one of several catalogues of galaxies.
These co-ordinates can then be plotted on whatever star atlas you are
using. From here, we go directly to locating the correct field of view
through our telescope. This may not always be as easy as it appears.

Once the correct field of view is located, and the anonymous galaxy is
seen, an accurate drawing of the objects in the field should be made,
showing the galaxy in relation to the field stars. It is also advisable
to show the co-ordinates of the galaxy, as determined in the preplanning,
somewhere near the field drawing. Besides an accurate drawing a complete
written description should be made.

After the observing session, the observer can take the field drawing
and written description and check them against the characteristics of the
galaxy as given in a catalogue. Catalogues suited for this purpose
include the Uppsala General Catalogue of Galaxies and the Morphological
Catalogue of Galaxies (although the latter is currently out of print).
Characteristics of the galaxy which should be checked include the shape,
i.e., if extended, orientation, type and visibility of its nucleus
(stellar or non-stellar), overall photographic magnitude, stars which may
be involved or close to the outer envelope, etc.....

Another useful aid the observer can use are photographs against which
field drawings can be checked. The P.O.S.S. prints are excellent for this
purpose. With the co-ordinates of the galaxy in question already known
it should be a simple matter to locate it on the appropriate P.O.S.S.
print. If your drawing accurately shows the field stars around the
anonymous galaxy, you should be able to use the prints to identify
positively the galaxy in your drawing. Although the brightness of some
stars will differ from your visual impression (since the P.O.S.S. prints
are either preferentially blue or red sensitive) the star patterns will
remain the same. It is important that you pay particular attention to
any unusual star patterns, such as 'star chains', circles, triangles, etc.
Be certain to include these details in your field drawing, even if they
are just outside the field. When comparing your drawing with a photo,
be sure to line up the north point of the drawing with the north point
photo as accurately as possible.

Sometimes a brighter deep-sky object, such as an NGC object or a
bright star, will be found within the same field as an anonymous galaxy.
This brighter object will act as a reference point and will simplify
identification of the galaxy in question. Of course, during the actual

Visual Observation

observing, the brighter object can be placed out of the field. Here again, as with the unusual star patterns, if the bright NGC object or star is located outside your field, it should nonetheless be indicated on your field drawing. One example might read: "NGC XXXX lies just under two fields of view north of this anonymous galaxy" (mention the power used or field size). If you do use a 'bright' star as a reference point and this star is too faint to be listed on the atlas you are using, try checking the AAVSO or SAO star atlases.

If two or more anonymous galaxies are seen in the same field the procedure will basically be the same as for a single galaxy seen in the field. I have found that the Catalogue of Galaxies and Clusters of Galaxies (CGCG), in 6 volumes, by Zwicky, is a great aid in identifying small groups of anonymous galaxies. The CGCG not only lists the galaxies as seen on the P.O.S.S. prints but also includes a map showing the relative positions of these galaxies. The CGCG gives the observer a positive method for identifying particular galaxies as seen on the P.O.S.S. prints.

Sometimes a photograph will show five galaxies or more in a small group, but the observer sees just two or three in the same field. The positions of these galaxies relative to each other and/or relative to a reference object is very important. The field drawing should be as accurate as possible. Once we have a field drawing and a set of verbal descriptions we need to check the characteristics of all the galaxies in question, as compared to their characteristics as listed in the catalogues. One important characteristic is that of the object's photographic magnitude. If the catalogues list two galaxies close to each other, of Mp 14.0 and 15.0, but the observer sees only one object, the chances are that it was the brightest which was seen.

Remember that an accurate field drawing and a complete verbal description of the object, made at the eyepiece, are two of the best tools an observer can use when trying to identify an anonymous galaxy. The more accurate the drawing and the more complete the description the easier the identification process will be.

For observers who find drawing at the telescope a difficult procedure, there is an alternative – a detailed tape recording of each observation, including unambiguous comments on the location, relative brightness and appearance of each object in the field, together with time, magnification and other relevant details. Modern tape recorders are small and can be operated with a single press button thus leaving the hands free and, since no light is needed, dark adaption is preserved. Written notes and drawings could be compiled the next day. For the perfectionist, both a drawing at the telescope and an audio-record can be made!

PART TWO

CATALOGUE OF OBSERVATIONS

Catalogue

Introduction

This catalogue contains a record of observations of 165 anonymous galaxies made by only two observers, the authors of this book. In previous volumes of the Handbook contributions by a large number of observers, using a wide variety of instruments, were included. The observation of anonymous galaxies, however, is a new and specialised field for the amateur and has been pioneered almost exclusively by Thomson and Morales. As the scope for discovery of new objects in this class is virtually unlimited, the sample presented here is likely to be only the first of many such compilations.

The majority of the observations (137) was made by MJT with the 16½-inch (42 cm.) reflector of Westmont College Observatory, which has been described in the Introduction to Part One. The remainder (28) were observed by RJM with two telescopes, a 17½-inch (44.5 cm.), f/4.5 Coulter Dobsonian, and a similar instrument of 13.1-inch (33.3 cm.) aperture. One object, MCG -2-14-004 (A018), was also observed with a 10-inch (25.4 cm) f/5.6 Newtonian. This work was carried out at the Sonoran Desert Observatory, which is located some 35 miles north of Old Mexico, to the east of Kitt Peak. This site enjoys a high frequency of clear skies and excellent seeing conditions.

The Catalogue

The Catalogue is divided into the following Sections:

Section 1

Upper Line:
(a) W.S. No. As the Catalogue is the first – and so far the only one – of its kind and contains some objects entirely unlisted in other publications, some sequential numbering is essential for easy reference. No proprietary claim by the Webb Society is implied, however!
(b) Name. References to other catalogues, descriptions of which are covered in Chapter 2.
(c) Positions. R.A. and Dec. are given for Epoch 1950.0. All of the catalogues referred to, and most of the atlases in general use, are for this Epoch. Positions for Epoch 2000.0 are given in Section 3.
(d) The symbol * indicates that a field drawing of the object will be found in Section 2.
Field Diagrams:
These are merely locating diagrams, mostly taken from the relevant

Catalogue

P.O.S.S. prints. The area covered in each view may vary, but the scale can be estimated from the data given under 'Observation'. In some cases a smaller scale (larger field diameter) is employed in order to include an identifiable NGC object.

Section 2 - Selected Telescope Field Drawings.

Twenty-nine actual drawings made at the telescope by RJM. Details of telescope/eyepiece combination used, orientation and field diameter are included.

Section 3 - Positions for Epoch 2000.0.

. . . .

The following objects should not be difficult to see visually in telescopes of 12-inch (30.5 cm.) aperture:

Name	R.A.	Dec.	Mag.
MCG -02-14-004	05 09.3	-14 52	13.5 (p)
MCG +05-19-001 UGC 03995	07 41.0	+29 21	13.6 (p)
MCG +03-30-066 UGC 06697	11 41.2	+20 15	14.3 (p)
MCG +09-17-027 UGC 05459	10 04.9	+53 19	13.8 (p)

W.S. No.	Name	R.A. (1950) Dec.	Telescope
A 001	UGC 00065	00 05.4 +32 43	16½-inch

Observation: lies 84" of R.A. p. and 15 arc-min S. of NGC 20.
Close f. are 4 stars aligned N-S, UGC 00065 is N.p. southernmost.
References: MCG - not listed. UGC - 00065, Mkn 338, 1'.1 x 0'.7,
Mp 13.8. CGCG - Anon., Mp 13.8, ZWG 499.051. POSS - plate 0-1257
elliptical, sl. el. N.p.-S.f., v. sm. envelope.

A 002	Unlisted	00 46.1 +31 42	16½-inch

Observation: R.A. & Dec. apply to NGC 262, just S.p. A 002, which
is ex. faint and seen only with a.v. Distance from NGC 262 is
less than half that separating NGC 262 from a daint star S.f.
References: MCG & CGCG - not listed. UGC - listed in notes as
comp. to NGC 262, 0'.5 x 0'.5, P.A. 86°, 1'.2 dist. RNGC - listed
as comp. to NGC 262. POSS - plate 0-601, ex. small, almost stell.

A 003	MCG 7-3-31	01 18.2 +40 12	16½-inch

Observation: 12" of R.A. p. and 1 arc-min S. of NGC 477.
Irregular, small and faint. Sl. el. S.p.-N.f.? Seen well at x351.
Of similar mag. to star off S. tip of NGC 477.
References: MCG - 7-3-31, Fc, Mp 14.0. UGC - in notes; 0'.8 x
0'.45, spiral, Mp 14.8. CGCG - Anon., Mp 14.8, ZWG 536.030.
RNGC - comp. S.p. NGC 477. POSS - plate 0-627, sl. el., major
axis as described, eccentric nuc., located towards f. edge.

A 004	MCG 5-4-48	01 21.1 +33 04	16½-inch

Observation: 18" of R.A. f. and 4 arc-min N. of NGC 507, the
dominant member of a small cluster, also incl. NGC 508. N.f. NGC
508 are two stars of equal mag., aligned N.p.-S.f.; A 003 lies f.
northernmost of these. Irregular, medium size, brighter towards
centre. Well seen at x351.
References: MCG - 5-4-48, Nme, Mp 16.0. UGC - not listed. CGCG -
Anon., Mp 15.0, ZWG 502.702. POSS - plate 0-30, compact, small
diff. env., fainter comp. close N.

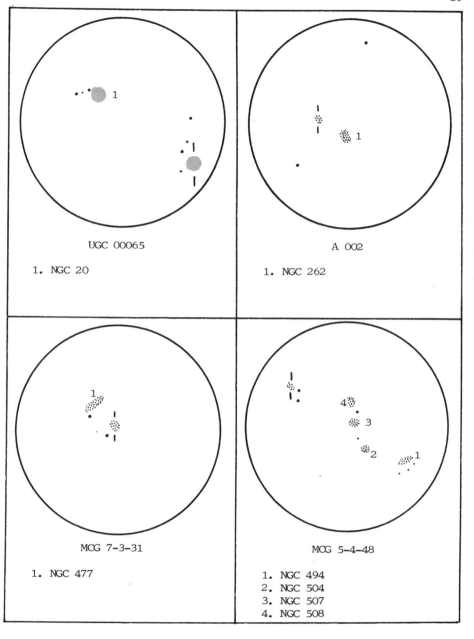

UGC 00065

1. NGC 20

A 002

1. NGC 262

MCG 7-3-31

1. NGC 477

MCG 5-4-48

1. NGC 494
2. NGC 504
3. NGC 507
4. NGC 508

W.S. No.	Name	R.A. (1950) Dec.		Telescope

A 005 UGC 06528 01 29.9 +62 07 16½-inch

Observation: lies 54" of R.A. p. and 3 arc-min S. of NGC 3725.
Easily visible and similar to NGC 3725; oval, no nuc. and uniform
surface brightness.
References: MCG – 10-17-13, Bw, 2 wc, Di, Mp 14.0. UGC – 06528,
Sc, 1'.2 x 1'.1, Mp 14.1. CGCG – Anon., Mp 14.1. POSS – plate
O-723, bright centre with stell. nuc. in tight spiral arms.

A 006 UGC 01866 02 22.0 +41 38 13.1-inch*

Observation: forms trio with NGC 910 & 912; slightly smaller than
910 but easier. Very bright core in fainter envelope, poss. el.
S.p.-N.f., patchy appearance. 2 f. stars close to N. edge.
References: MCG – 7-6-11, L, 2 a, Mp 15.0. UGC – 01866, 1'.1 x
x 0'.6, SBa, P.A. 30°, Mp 14.9. CGCG – Anon., Mp 14.9. POSS –
plate O-449, sm., sl. el., thin outer env., brighter middle.

A 007 MCG 5-7-17 02 31.8 +32 38 16½-inch

Observation: listed with same co-ordinates as NGC 978. Observed
at Westmont, MCG 5-7-17 appeared as a v. faint 'star' or 'knot'
on f. edge of NGC 978.
References: MCG – 5-7-17, N, 2 aw, Mp 15.0. UGC – in notes; comp.
to NGC 978. CGCG – double system with NGC 978. POSS – plate
O-1301, attached to S.f. end of NGC 978. Gives impression of
being in front of outer arms of NGC 978. Poss. el. N.p.-S.f.

A 008 UGC 02126 02 35.6 +40 30 16½-inch

Observation: 30" of R.A. p. and 10 arc-min S. of NGC 1003. Faint,
medium size, irregularly round. Star visible in N.p. edge.
References: MCG – 7-6-46, P, Lab, Mp 15.0. UGC – 02126, 1'.4 x
1'.4, Sab, Mp 15.4. CGCG – Anon., diff., Mp 15.4. POSS – plate
O-449, small round spot of nebulosity with brighter centre. A
star just off p. edge is easily visible.

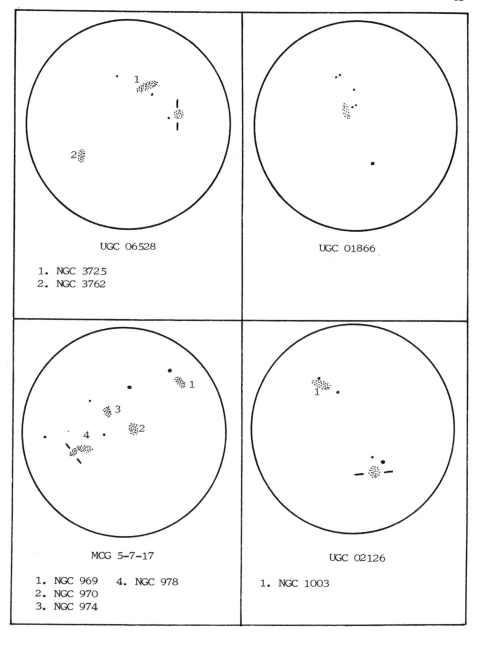

UGC 06528

1. NGC 3725
2. NGC 3762

UGC 01866

MCG 5-7-17

1. NGC 969   4. NGC 978
2. NGC 970
3. NGC 974

UGC 02126

1. NGC 1003

W.S. No.	Name	R.A. (1950)	Dec.	Telescope

A 009   MCG 1-9-41   03 27.6   -05 42   16½-inch

Observation: 6" of R.A. p. and 1 arc-min N. of NGC 1346. At x351, barely visible, very narrow and quite long, el. N-S. Lies N. of a point between NGC 1346 and a star p.
References: MCG - 1-9-41, Fb, extended, Mp 16.0. UGC & CGCG - not listed. RNGC - listed in notes as elongated comp., close N. POSS - plate O-1456, el., small nuc., f. edge of major axis looks disturbed with short 'flares' or 'jets'.

A 010   UGC 02927   03 58.7   +22 58   16½ & 13.1-inch*

Observation: 16½ = lies 24" of R.A. p. and 2 arc-min S. of NGC 1497. Apex 'star' of a small triangle p. NGC 1497 seems neb., especially on p. side. With x176 and x351, nebular image strong. 13.1 = at x147 not bright but seen with direct vision. Small, faint, of uncertain form. V. diff. with compact br. nuc. Two obvious stars p., northernmost brighter. Not seen with x94.
References: MCG - 4-10-6, N, Db+*, Mp 15.2. UGC - 02927, 2'.4 x 1'.5, P.A. 80°, SBa, Mp 15.2. CGCG - Anon., Mp 15.2, ZWG 487.007. POSS - plate O-31, ex. diff., on p. side of star. Sl. el. S.p.- N.f. Stell. nuc. & ex. faint spiral arms.

A 011   UGC 02931   03 59.3   +25 40   13.1-inch*

Observation: at x147, v. faint patch, even brightness. S. of central of 3 stars in field. Small nuc. susp. at x187; difficult.
References: MCG - 4-10-10, Na, Da, Mp 15.0. UGC - 02931, 1'.4 x 1'.0, P.A. 15°, Sc, Mp 14.8. CGCG - Anon., ZWG 487.011, Mp 14.8. POSS - plate O-31, sm., round, br. middle. Star on N.f. edge.

A 012   UGC 02949   04 02.0   +25 07   13.1-inch*

Observation: with x147, just vis. in same field as NGC 1508. Of similar brightness to NGC 1508 but smaller, ell. and uniform surface br. At x187, el. p.-f., no nuc. V. faint with x94.
References: MCG - 4-10-19, F+F, Mp 15.0. UGC - 02949, 1'.2 x 0'.6, P.A. 119°, SBab, Mp 14.6. CGCG - Anon., ZWG 487.019, Mp 14.6. POSS - plate O-31, sm., el. N.p.-S.f., outer envelope uniformly bright.

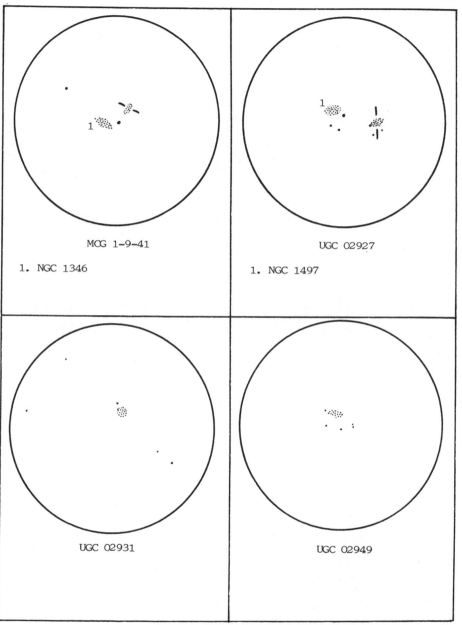

MCG 1-9-41

1. NGC 1346

UGC 02927

1. NGC 1497

UGC 02931

UGC 02949

W.S. No.	Name	R.A. (1950) Dec.		Telescope

A 013 MCG 12-5-6 04 28.2 +73 11 16½-inch

Observation: first of 3, and faintest of group, led by NGC 1573.
72" of R.A. p. and 2 arc-min N. of NGC 1573. Small and very
diffuse. Double star lies close N.p.
References: MCG - 12-5-6, 2 Ƶ at, Mp 15.0. UGC - noted as comp.
N.p. NGC 1573, 0'.8 x 0'.35, spiral, Mp 15.5. CGCG - Anon., Mp
15.5. RNGC - comp. 3' N.p. NGC 1573. POSS - plate 0-866, small,
diamond-shaped, stell. nuc., major axis S.p.-N.f.

A 014 MCG 12-5-7 04 28.4 +73 06 16½-inch

Observation: second of 3, with MCG 12-5-6 (above) and NGC 1573.
48" of R.A. p. and 3 arc-min S. of NGC 1573. Small, very faint
and brighter in centre. N.p. is a triangle of faint stars.
References: MCG - 12-5-7, E, Mp 15.0. UGC - 03069, ell., 1'.3 x
0'.7, Mp 15.1. CGCG - Anon., Mp 15.1. RNGC - comp. S.p. NGC
1573. POSS -plate 0-866, small, sl.el. S.p.-N.f., br. middle.

A 015 MCG 0-12-51 04 33.7 -02 57 13.1-inch*

Observation: first of 2. Easy with direct vision at x94. Round,
small, diffuse env. with poss. central brightening. At x147 it
appears a little extended. Faint star f.
References: MCG - 0-12-51, N, 2 a, Mp 14.8. UGC - not listed.
CGCG - Anon., ZWG 393.044, Mp 14.8. POSS - plate 0-1524, small
extended N.p.-S.f., v. faint glow around envelope.

A 016 MCG 0-12-54 04 33.9 -02 59 13.1-inch*

Observation: second of 2, with MCG 0-12-51 (above). Smaller and
fainter than companion but easily visible at x94. Round. Noted
to have a bright, condensed (possibly stellar) core at x147,
outer envelope easy to see.
References: MCG - 0-12-54, Ne(N), Mp 14.0. UGC - not listed.
CGCG - Anon., ZWG 393.045, Mp 14.8. POSS - plate 0-1524, smaller
than MCG 0-12-51, extended S.S.p.-N.N.f. Uniform brightness
throughout.

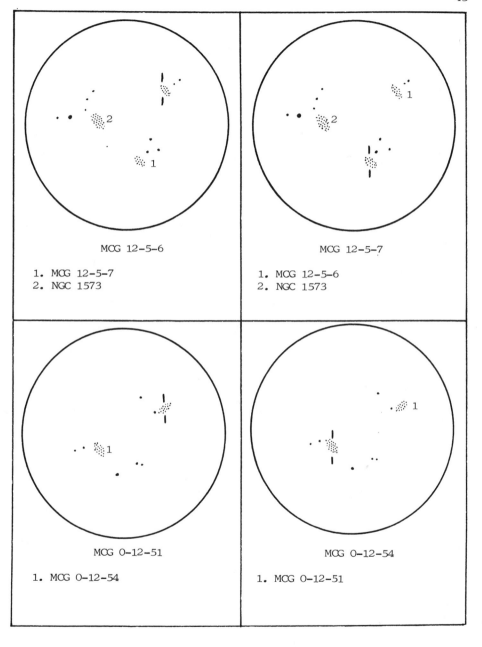

MCG 12-5-6

1. MCG 12-5-7
2. NGC 1573

MCG 12-5-7

1. MCG 12-5-6
2. NGC 1573

MCG 0-12-51

1. MCG 0-12-54

MCG 0-12-54

1. MCG 0-12-51

W.S. No.	Name	R.A. (1950) Dec.		Telescope
A 017	UGC 03141	04 40.5	+00 38	16½-inch

Observation: 12" of R.A. f. and 8 arc-min N. of NGC 1642. Faint, medium size, irregular, no visible nucleus. Faint star near N.f. edge; group of 4 stars form wide trapezium further N.
References: MCG - 0-12-73, n, Da, 2sa, Mp 15.0. UGC - 03141, 1'.0 x 1'.0, Mp 15.3. CGCG - Anon., Mp 15.3. POSS - plate O-1524, small diffuse spiral, stellar nuc. has a bright knot in N.f. end of outer structure. Very faint arms.

A 018	MCG -2-14-004	05 09.3	-14 52	13.1 & 10-inch*

Observation: easy to see, noticed with direct vision at x94. Large, faintish, irreg. round and gradually brighter towards the centre. A.v. suggests major axis extended N-S. Listed in Second Catalogue of Galaxies (de Vaucouleurs et al.) as A0509-14.
References: MCG - -2-14-004, Le, 2Sssb, Mp 13.1. UGC & CGCG - not listed. POSS - plate O-1520, outer envelope is faint, oval, sl. extended E-W. Spiral arms noted. Brighter condensed nuc.

A 019	UGC 03803	07 17.0	+22 11	13.1-inch*

Observation: seen with a.v. at x94 after 55 Gem. was placed just outside the field. Roundish, faint, patch of light. Even brightness. Difficult. UGC 04096 = IC 480.
References: MCG - 4-18-002, N, Da 1 ifa, Mp 15.1. UGC - 03803, 1'.0 x 0'.9, Sa, Mp 15.1. CGCG - Anon., Mp 15.1. POSS - plate O-1310, very small outer envelope, even brightness, close to a bright star SAO 079294.

A 020	UGC 03827	07 20.2	+22 18	13.1-inch*

Observation: lies 42" of R.A. f. and 8 arc-min N. of NGC 2365. At x147 resembles miniature Merope nebula because of obvious star on S.f. edge. Round. Best observed with a.v. but can be seen with direct vision; noted with a.v. at x94.
References: MCG - 4-18-013, (N), 2Sb+*, Mp 14.8. UGC - 03827, 1'.1 x 1'.1, SB?, Mp 14.8. CGCG - Anon., ZWG 117.029, Mp 14.8. POSS - plate O-1310, irreg. round, small outer envelope, brighter core seen to be extended.

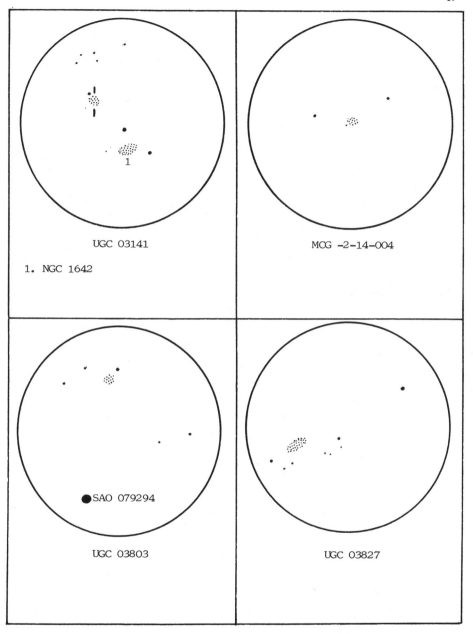

UGC 03141

MCG -2-14-004

1. NGC 1642

SAO 079294

UGC 03803

UGC 03827

W.S. No.	Name	R.A. (1950) Dec.	Telescope

A 021   UGC 03937   07 34.3   +35 43 $16\frac{1}{2}$-inch

Observation: quite easily visible at x84. Oval, no nuc. visible,
gradual increase in brightness to centre. At x176, star seen
just off p. extension. 2 bright stars S.p. at a distance,
aligned N.p.-S.f., p. star brighter.
References: MCG - 6-17-023, L, 22b, Mp 14.0. UGC - 03937, 2'.1 x
0'.5, Type SB?, P.A. 151°, Mp 14.2. CGCG - Anon., Mp 14.2. POSS
plate O-1336, elongated, no nuc. but main brightening of lens is
towards S.p. end.

A 022   UGC 03944   07 35.2   +37 45 $16\frac{1}{2}$-inch

Observation: V. faint but visible at x84. Elongated N.p.-S.f.,
appearing as small, uniform streak of light. At x176, central
area brightening noted. At x351, faint star noted in p. end.
Close double lies N.f., components aligned E-W, f. brightest.
References: MCG - 6-17-024, L?, RLc?, 2bf, Mp 14.0. UGC - 03944,
2'.0 x 0'.9, Sc, P.A. 130°, Mp 15.0. CGCG - Anon., Mp 15.0.
POSS - plate O-1336, stell. nuc. in oval lens with 2 faint spiral
arms, N.p.-S.f.

A 023   UGC 03995   07 41.0   +29 21   13.1-inch*

Observation: easily seen at x94 as faint patch with slightly
brighter centre. El. E-W. At x147 core brighter, perhaps stell.,
and offset towards f. end of envelope, like a comet.
References: MCG - 5-19-001, L, 1Sa, 1Sa Na, Dab, Mp 13.6. UGC -
03995, 2'.5 x 1'.1, P.A. 85°, Pec., Mp 13.6. CGCG - Anon., ZWG
148.037, Mp 13.6. POSS - plate O-1344, fairly large, extended
E-W. Some spiral structure, 2 arms and br. bar form major axis.

A 024   UGC 04014   07 43.2   +74 27 $16\frac{1}{2}$-inch

Observation: first of 4 anon. galaxies in field. Moderately br.,
v. compact, difficult to distinguish from a star even using x422.
References: MCG - 12-8-11, E?, Mp 15.0. UGC - 04014, 1'.0 x 0'.5,
P.A. 122°, E-SO, Mp 14.4. CGCG - Anon., Mp 14.4. POSS - plate
O-680, small el. system, N.p.-S.f. Brighter lens with diffuse
outer envelope.

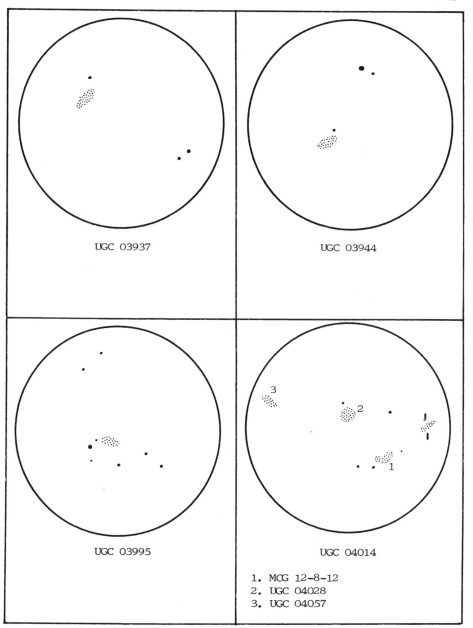

UGC 03937

UGC 03944

UGC 03995

UGC 04014

1. MCG 12-8-12
2. UGC 04028
3. UGC 04057

W.S. No.	Name	R.A. (1950) Dec.		Telescope

| A 025 | UGC 04028 | 07 44.8 | +74 28 | 16½-inch |

Observation: third in field. Moderately br., irregularly round, poss. a little el. S.p.-N.f., small, of uniform brightness. At x176, el. confirmed and slightly brighter centre noted. Nucleus offset to S. end. Fairly br. star N.p., faint star close p.
References: MCG - 12-8-13, BR?, 2Scm, Mp 13.0. UGC - 04028, 1'.1 x 1'.0, P.A. 10°, SAB, Mp 12.7. CGCG - Anon., Mp 12.7. POSS - plate O-680, br. face-on spiral with prominent S-shaped arms enclosed in a circular envelope.

| A 026 | MCG 5-19-10 | 07 45.8 | +29 01 | 13.1-inch* |

Observation: difficult. First noticed with a.v. at x147. Seen with direct vision at x187 but v. faint. Irregularly round with suggestion of brighter mid-region.
References: MCG 5-19-10, N:H, Mp 15.2. UGC - not listed. CGCG - Anon., ZWG 148.031, Mp 15.2. POSS - plate O-1344, v. small, round, faint outer envelope, brighter condensed lens.

| A 027 | MCG 12-8-14 | 07 46.0 | +72 09 | 16½-inch |

Observation: p. of 2; found while observing UGC 04050 at x176. Smaller and fainter than UGC 04050. Irregular. No central brightening. At x351, v.f. star visible close S.p.
References: MCG - 12-8-14, (N), Mp 17.0. UGC & CGCG - not listed. POSS - plate O-680, v. small, v. faint, el. N.p.-S.f. Brighter lens in envelope of small extent.

| A 028 | UGC 04038 | 07 46.5 | +27 02 | 13.1-inch* |

Observation: difficult, visibility made worse by conspicuous star on S.f. edge. UGC 04038 is faint, elliptical, extended E-W, nuc. suspected. Observed with a.v. at x187.
References: MCG - 5-19-13, Fa, Mp 15.1. UGC - 04038, 1'.1 x 0'.4, P.A. 83°, Mp 15.1. CGCG - Anon., ZWG 148.037, Mp 15.1. POSS - plate O-1344, sm., extended S.S.p.-N.N.f. Envelope of uniform surface brightness.

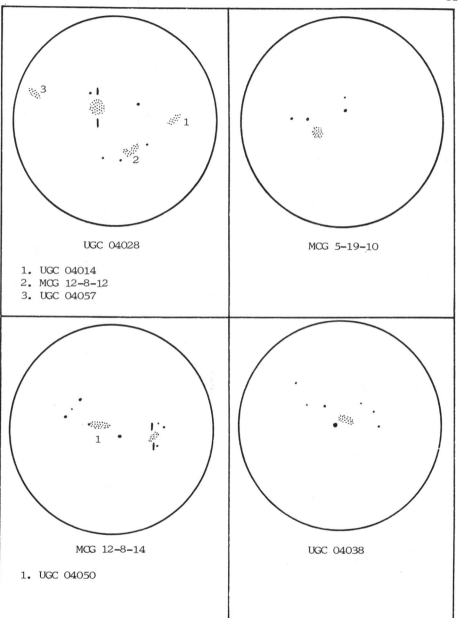

UGC 04028

1. UGC 04014
2. MCG 12-8-12
3. UGC 04057

MCG 5-19-10

MCG 12-8-14

1. UGC 04050

UGC 04038

W.S. No.	Name	R.A. (1950) Dec.	Telescope

| A 029 | UGC 04041 | 07 46.7 +73 38 | 16½-inch |

Observation: small and considerably elongated N.p.-S.f., centre brightening to extended nucleus with star close to tip of p. extension. Easy at x84. Beautiful edge-on at x351, extensions narrowing to points, star p. prominent.
References: MCG – 12-8-16, L, (2S), Mp 15.0. UGC – 04041, 1'.0 x 0'.35, S, Mp 13.6. Listed in notes as early type spiral, P.A. 132°. CGCG – Anon., Mp 13.6. POSS – plate O-680, bright,ext. Brighter in central area to an extended nucleus.

| A 030 | UGC 04050 | 07 47.3 +72 10 | 16½-inch |

Observation: f. MCG 12-8-14 (A 027). Small, faint, oval, and noted to be sl. brighter in the centre at x176. At x351, appears to widen at p. end. Major axis S.p.-N.f., pointing towards the brightest of 3 stars N.f. Bright star S.p.
References: MCG – 12-8-17, (N), Mp 15.0. UGC – 04050, 0'.7 x 0'.6 S?, Mp 14.3. CGCG – Anon., Mp 14.3. POSS – plate O-680, small tear-shaped object with p. end wider. Star superimposed on f. end. Lens slightly eccentric towards p. end.

| A 031 | MCG 12-8-12 | 07 47.6 +74 26 | 16½-inch |

Observation: directly S. of a faint star between UGC 04014 and UGC 04028. V. small, irreg. round, extremely difficult. Glimpsed with x351 when an e.f. star precedes it.
References: MCG – 12-8-12, L?, Db, (S'), Mp 16.0. UGC – listed in notes to UGC 04014 as double system (0'.9 x 0'.4 & 0'.5 x 0'.4), separated by 0'.45, Mp 15.6. CGCG – Anon., Mp 15.6. POSS – plate O-680, small, diamond-shaped, stell. nuc., comp. on S.f. edge.

| A 032 | UGC 04057 | 07 48.0 +74 32 | 16½-inch |

Observation: El. S.p.-N.f., brighter and wider in centre. Nuc. quite bright, poss. stell., at x176. Extensions narrow at each end. Star seen close f.
References: MCG 12-8-18, Ne)Da Raf., Mp 14.0. UGC – 04057, 2'.6 x 0'.7, P.A. 55°, Sa, Mp 13.4. CGCG – not listed. POSS – plate O-680, stell. nuc. in br. ext. lens in large el. envelope.

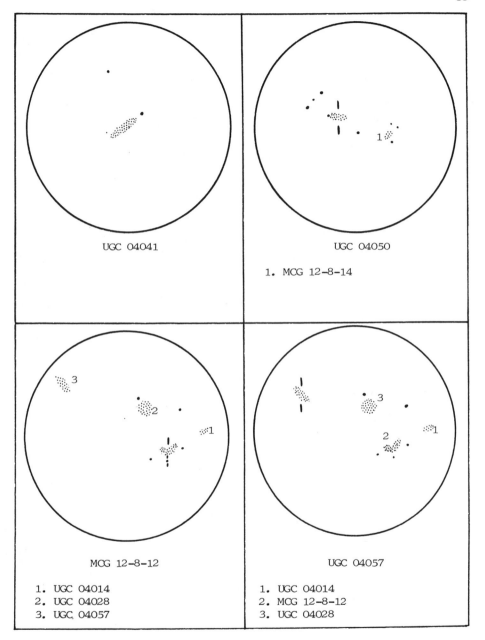

UGC 04041

UGC 04050

1. MCG 12-8-14

MCG 12-8-12

1. UGC 04014
2. UGC 04028
3. UGC 04057

UGC 04057

1. UGC 04014
2. MCG 12-8-12
3. UGC 04028

W.S. No.	Name	R.A. (1950) Dec.		Telescope
A 033	UGC 04122	07 54.8	+59 15	16½-inch

Observation: v. faint, small, el. N.p.-S.f. but visible at x84.
Central brightening noted at x176. Star close N.f. and beyond
this two stars aligned N.p.-S.f., p. being the brighter.
References: MCG - 10-12-40, E, Mp 14.0. UGC - 04122, 1'.6 x 1'.1,
E, Mp 14.7. CGCG - Anon., dbl. with UGC 04124, Mp 14.7. POSS -
plate O-960, small, oval, br. centre with a small lens sl.
extended almost N-S. Fainter envelope surrounds.

A 034	UGC 04124	07 54.9	+59 17	16½-inch

Observation: lies close N.f. UGC 04122. First noticed at x351.
Seen only as a small, faint nebulous knot just N. of a star close
to N.f. edge of UGC 04122.
References: MCG - 10-12-14, N, 2sa, Da, Mp 16.0. UGC - 04124,
1'.1 x 0'.9, SO, Mp 15.4. CGCG - Anon., double system in halo,
Mp 15.4. POSS - plate O-960, small, el. N.p.-S.f., brighter nuc.

A 035	UGC 04241	08 05.3	+57 55	16½-inch

Observation: 36 sec. of R.A. f. and on same Dec. as NGC 2521.
El. N.p.-S.f., uniform surface brightness but poss. slight
brightening offset towards p. end. Faint star S. of p. extension,
star of similar mag. f. following extension.
References: MCG - 10-12-80, La, Mp 14.0. UGC - 04241, 1'.1 x 0'.4
Sa-b, Mp 14.8. CGCG - Anon., with faint jet, Mp 14.8. POSS -
plate O-960, el., stell. nuc., 'jet' may be edge-on galaxy. Faint
star superimposed on f. extension.

A 036	MCG 7-18-18A	08 29.8	+41 16	16½-inch

Observation: first of 3, with UGC 04465 & 04468. Small, round,
brightening in centre to small nuc. Lies within a Sagitta-like
figure. Small, even, envelope visible at x422.
References: MCG - 7-18-18A, (N), H, Mp 14.0. UGC - not listed.
CGCG - Anon., Mp 14.9. POSS - plate O-707, compact, small lens
with small diffuse outer envelope.

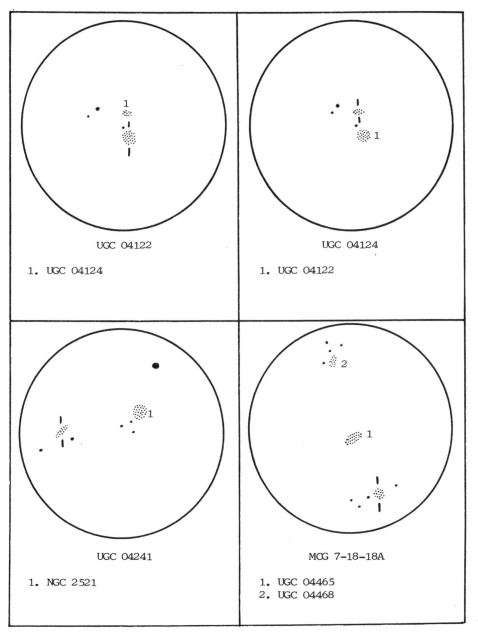

UGC 04122

1. UGC 04124

UGC 04124

1. UGC 04122

UGC 04241

1. NGC 2521

MCG 7-18-18A

1. UGC 04465
2. UGC 04468

W.S. No.	Name	R.A.	(1950)	Dec.	Telescope

A 037   UGC 04465   08 30.0   +41 26   16½-inch

Observation: 2nd of two. Easily visible at x84 when it is very
small, circular, stell. nuc., surrounded by small envelope of
uniform surface brightness. Very bright star S.f.
References: MCG - 7-18-19, (N)?, H, Mp 14.0. UGC - 04465, 1'.2 x
0'.8, Sa, Mp 15.0. CGCG - Anon., Mp 15.0. POSS - plate 0-707,
small br. lens with diffuse envelope, little extended N.p.-S.f.

A 038   UGC 04468   08 30.2   +41 42   16½-inch

Observation: 3rd of 3. Fairly bright and largest of 3. El. N.p.-
S.f. At x351 extended major axis well seen and the brighter nuc.
is also found to be extended. S. extension seems to narrow more
than N. Coarse double star close N.f., components N.p.-S.f.
References: MCG - 7-18-20, E?, Mp 14.0. UGC - 04468, 1'.5 x 0'.9,
SO, P.A. 165°, Mp 14.7. CGCG - Anon., Mp 14.7. POSS - plate
0-707, el. as described, central lens also el. N.p.-S.f.

A 039   UGC 04498   08 34.0   +40 13   16½-inch

Observation: V. small, circular, stell. nuc., easily visible at
x84. With x176, stell. nuc. prominent, envelope of even extent.
Trapezium of stars close p. with another star in the centre. UGC
04498 lies just N. of the f. star of this group.
References: MCG - 7-18-30, N, H, Mp 14.0. UGC - 04498, 1'.1 x
0'.7, P.A. 10°, SBa, Mp 14.8. CGCG - Anon., Mp 14.8. POSS -
plate 0-707, small lens with diffuse small envelope.

A 040   UGC 04572   08 42.4   +37 07   16½-inch

Observation: With x176, v. small, fairly bright, circular. Not
seen with x84. At x422, appears as small compact system of
uniform surface brightness. Faint star close N.f. and 2 stars of
similar mag. S.f. V.f. star ⅓ dist. from N.f. star to galaxy.
References: MCG - 6-19-21, (N)?, H, Mp 14.0. UGC - 04572, 0'.7 x
0'.7, compact, Mp 13.8. CGCG - Anon., Mp 13.8. POSS - plate
0-648, small elliptical with brighter central area.

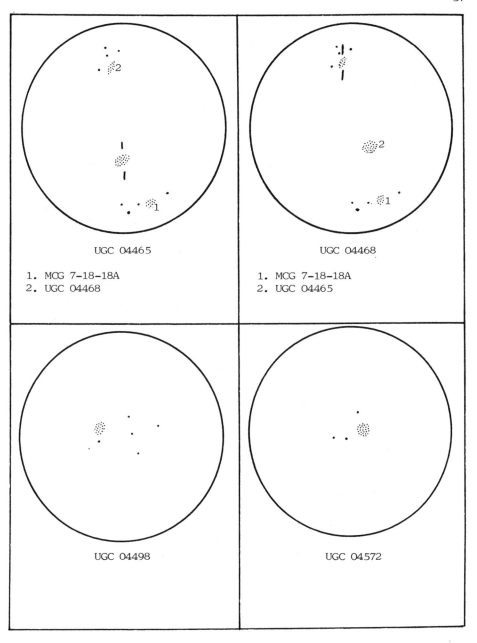

UGC 04465

1. MCG 7-18-18A
2. UGC 04468

UGC 04468

1. MCG 7-18-18A
2. UGC 04465

UGC 04498

UGC 04572

W.S. No.	Name	R.A. (1950) Dec.		Telescope

A 041   UGC 04633   08 48.5   +53 04   16½-inch

Observation: Not seen with x84 and only just detected with x176;
best seen with x351. Extremely faint, small, uniformly bright,
irregular in shape. Makes a triangle with 2 faint stars of
similar mag. which lie p. and S.p.
References: MCG - 9-15-36, L:Db:1, :1scm, Mp 15.0. UGC - 04633,
1'.1 x 0'.5, SBb, P.A. 87°, Mp 15.5. CGCG - Anon., Mp 15.5.
POSS - plate O-982, small, el. E-W, stell. nuc., brighter f. end.

A 042   UGC 04639   08 49.1   +17 08   16½-inch

Observation: visible at x84. Small, compact, irreg. round, seems
to brighten a little to centre. Lies S.f. the fainter (p.) of 2
stars aligned S.p.-N.f.
References: MCG - 3-23-15, (N)?, H, Mp 14.5. UGC - 04639, 1'.4 x
1'.3, S0?, Mp 14.5. CGCG - Anon., Mp 14.5. POSS - plate O-62.

A 043   MCG 8-16-36   08 51.4   +49 19   16½-inch

Observation: lies 6 sec. of R.A. and 1 arc-min S. of NGC 2684.
First noticed with x351; faint and very diffuse.
References: MCG - 8-16-36, N:, Mp 16.0. UGC - Notes mention a
group of small galaxies p. NGC 2684. This is incorrect as they
lie f. CGCG - not listed. POSS - plate O-671, small, almost
stell. nuc. with an ovaloid env. which involves a star close f.

A 044   MCG 8-16-37   08 51.5   +49 20   16½-inch

Observation: lies 12 sec. of R.A. f. and on same Dec. as NGC 2684.
Extremely faint; only glimpsed, f. star close S.f. NGC 2684.
References: MCG - 8-16-37, (Np), H, Mp 16.0. UGC & CGCG - not
listed. POSS - plate O-671, stellar. V. faint star (?) just off
N.p. edge. The object has a very small diffuse envelope. 'Star'
off N.p. edge possibly nebulous; double system ?

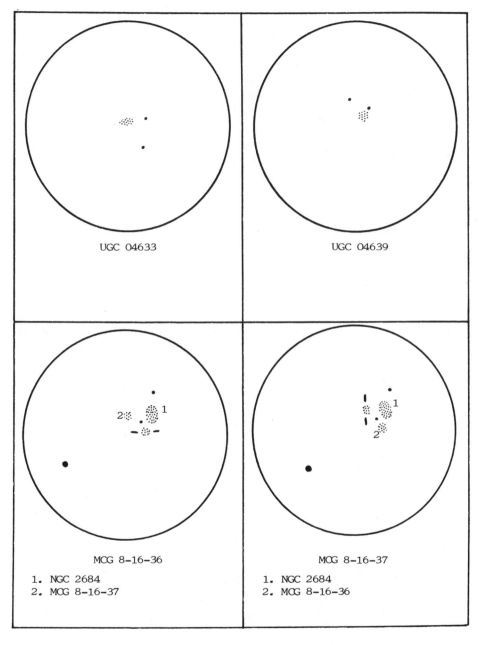

UGC 04633

UGC 04639

MCG 8-16-36

1. NGC 2684
2. MCG 8-16-37

MCG 8-16-37

1. NGC 2684
2. MCG 8-16-36

W.S. No.	Name	R.A. (1950) Dec.	Telescope

A 045 UGC 04713   08 56.7   +52 42   16½-inch

Observation: easily visible at x84. Quite bright, medium size, irreg. round, small br. nuc. surrounded by an envelope. Lies between 2 stars aligned N.p.-S.f.; a little closer to f. star. References: MCG - 0-15-70, L? bt., Mp 13.0. UGC - 04713, 1'.9 x 1'.3, Sb, Mp 13.7. CGCG - Anon., Mp 13.7. POSS - plate O-982, quite large, circular; stell. nuc. surrounded by a round env. which develops into faint outer spiral structure.

A 046 UGC 04717   08 57.0   +51 25   16½-inch

Observation: visble at x84 but v. small and v. faint; irregularly round and of uniform surface brightness. Better seen at x176 when it suggests being sl. el. S.p.-N.f. Star close f. while S.p. are 2 br. stars aligned E-W. Coarse dbl. lies S. of these. References: MCG - 9-15-73, (N), H, Mp 15.0. UGC - 04717, 1'.1 x 0'.5, Sa-b, P.A. 40°, Mp 15.1. CGCG - Anon., Mp 15.1. POSS - plate O-982, small spindle S.p.-N.f., brighter lens surrounded by a very small envelope.

A 047 MCG 6-20-18   08 57.1   +35 54   16½-inch

Observation: same R.A. and 30 arc-sec S. of NGC 2719. Appears as a small knot just separated from NGC 2719; small, not faint, easily visible and perhaps sl.el. N.p.-S.f. References: MCG - 6-20-18, Np+*, Mp 14.5. UGC - mentioned in notes to NGC 2719. CGCG - Anon., dbl. with NGC 2719. POSS - plate O-1342, small, ell., el. N.p.-S.f. Bright spot or star at each end.

A 048 UGC 04719   08 57.1   +50 53   16½-inch

Observation: obviously elongated, major axis E-W, brighter and wider on p. end. At x351 it is medium sized, poss. narrower on f. extension, certainly darker there. N. of a group of 4 stars of which brightest is directly S. Another star close S.p. References: MCG - 9-15-72, Fe, Mp 14.0. UGC - 04719, 2'.3 x 0'.3 Sc, Mp 15.0. CGCG - Anon., has faint comp., Mp 15.0. POSS - plate O-982, v. el. E-W, small nuc., p. extension brighter.

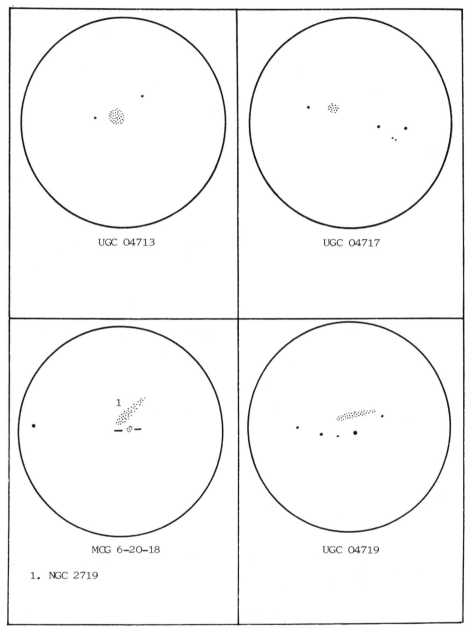

UGC 04713

UGC 04717

1

MCG 6-20-18

UGC 04719

1. NGC 2719

W.S. No.	Name	R.A. (1950) Dec.	Telescope
A 049	UGC 04730	08 58.0 +60 21	16½-inch

Observation: easily visible with x84. Small, faint, irregularly round, brightening in the centre. At x176, exhibits stell. nuc. in small envelope of uniform surface brightness. Star S.p. References: MCG – 10–13–52, (Nn), Mp 15.0. UGC – 04730, 0'.9 x 0'.3, P.A. 93°, Mp 14.3. CGCG – Anon., Mp 14.3. POSS – plate 0–1296, small spindle el. E–W. Small bright nucleus. Faint edge-on companion close N.p.

| A 050 | UGC 04775 | 09 03.3   +66 46 | 16½-inch |

Observation: at x84 it is faint, small, irreg. round and brighter in the middle to a small nucleus, and almost directly S. of a v. bright star, 17' distant. Easy with x176 when it appears small, with a v. br. stell. nuc. in a small, irreg. round envelope. References: MCG – 11–11–037, E?, r?, A?, Mp 15.0. UGC – 04775, 1'.4 x 0'.9, E–S0, Mp 14.3. CGCG – Anon., Mp 14.3. POSS – plate 0–1286, small br. lens with a faint env. extended N–S.

| A 051 | UGC 04867 | 09 11.5   +41 06 | 16½-inch |

Observation: lies 30 sec. of R.A. p. and 2 arc-min S. of NGC 2785. Large, faint, ill-defined object attached to southernmost of 3 stars p. NGC 2785. Best seen with x176 S.p. star. References: MCG – 7–19–39, Bpp?, 1 Sb, R, Db, Mp 14.0. UGC – 04867, 1'.9 x 1'.4, Mp 15.2. CGCG – Anon., Mp 15.2. RNGC – Notes section: very fragmented SB 5" S.p. POSS – plate 0–721, nice spiral with S-shaped arms, sl.el. S.p.–N.f., the star is invested in N.f. end.

| A 052 | UGC 04832 | 09 11.6   +79 19 | 16½-inch |

Observation: lies 1.4 min. of R.A. f. and 1 arc-min N. of NGC 2732. At x176, it is faint, el. N.p.–S.f., quite narrow and of uniform surface brightness. 'Arrowhead' of 4 stars just N. References: MCG – 13–7–17, F, Mp 15.0. UGC – 04832, 1'.5 x 0'.4, P.A. 118°, Pec., Mp 15.0. CGCG – Anon., Mp 15.0. POSS – plate 0–693, small, elongated, slight central brightening.

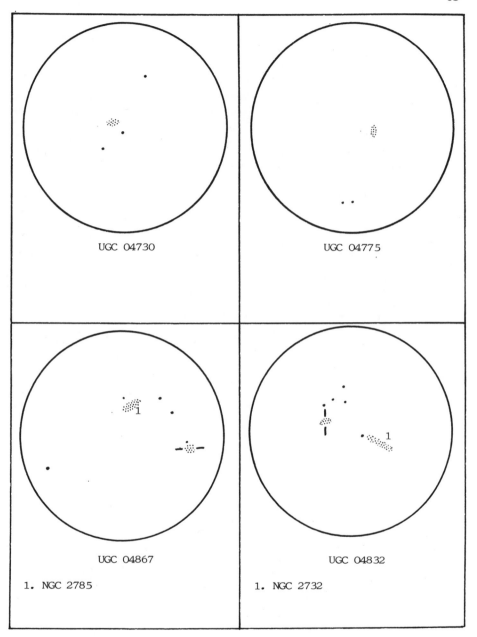

UGC 04730

UGC 04775

UGC 04867

1. NGC 2785

UGC 04832

1. NGC 2732

W.S. No.	Name	R.A. (1950) Dec.		Telescope
A 053	UGC 04904	09 14.0	+42 07	16½-inch

Observation: lies 6 sec. of R.A. p. and 5 arc-min S. of NGC 2798. Faint, medium size and appears extended N.p.-S.f. Uniform surface brightness. No additional detail visible at x351.
References: MCG - 7-19-54, (Np), H, Mp 14.0. UGC - 04904, 1'.1 x 0'.6, P.A. 137°, SB, Mp 15.0. CGCG - Anon., Mp 15.0. POSS - plate 0-721, el. N.p.-S.f., irregularly shaped envelope, bright curved arm in N. end forming arc.

A 054	MCG 6-21-24	09 17.8	+33 56	16½-inch

Observation: lies 1 minute of R.A. f. and 2 arc-min S. of NGC 2832. Faint, medium size, quite diffuse and irregular in shape. N.p. is the brightest star in field; a fainter star lies between.
References: MCG - 6-21-24, E?, Mp 15.0. UGC & CGCG - not listed. POSS - plate 0-925, elliptical with a small envelope. There is a very faint star on its S.p. edge.

A 055	Unlisted	09 21	-10 12	16½-inch

Observation: suspected at x176 and verified at x351, this object is 12 sec. of R.A. p. and on the same Dec. as NGC 2863. Very faint, small, sl.el. N.p.-S.f. A bright star lies p. and an e.f. star f. A line through the 3 objects points almost to the centre of NGC 2863.
References: MCG, UGC & CGCG - not listed. POSS - plate 0-1016, as described, between 2 stars. Small compact lens in small env.

A 056	ZWG 312.012	09 25.7	+62 46	16½-inch

Observation: on same R.A. and 3 arc-min N. of NGC 2880. Small, sl. el. S.p.-N.f. and brighter in the centre. Lies in a group of stars N.f. NGC 2880; nebular image contrasts well with the nearby stellar images.
References: MCG - not listed. UGC - in Notes; Mp 15.1. CGCG - Anon., ZWG 312.012, Mp 15.1. RNGC - noted in New Description as comp. N.f. NGC 2880. POSS - plate 0-708, v. compact, almost stellar. Easier to confirm telescopically than on plate.

65

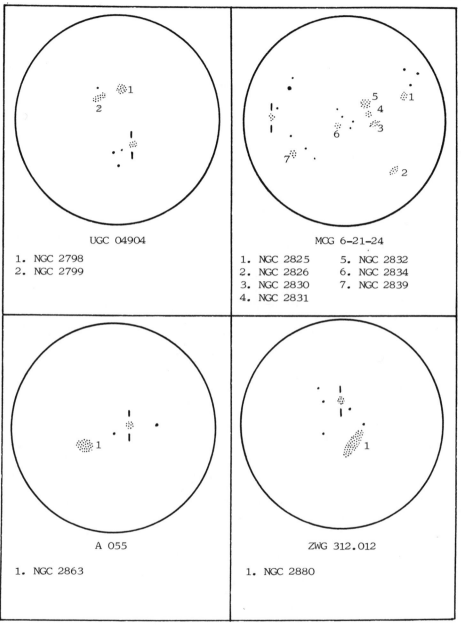

UGC 04904

1. NGC 2798
2. NGC 2799

MCG 6-21-24

1. NGC 2825   5. NGC 2832
2. NGC 2826   6. NGC 2834
3. NGC 2830   7. NGC 2839
4. NGC 2831

A 055

1. NGC 2863

ZWG 312.012

1. NGC 2880

W.S. No.	Name	R.A. (1950) Dec.	Telescope
A 057	UGC 05225	09 43.3 +46 00	16½-inch

Observation: best seen at x176 when seen to be compact and irreg. round. At x351, faint, v. small and of uniform surface brightness. V.f. star close f.; curved line of 3 stars S.p., aligned N–S.
References: MCG – 8–18–30, N, Da, Mp 15.0. UGC – 05225, 1'.1 x 1'.1, compact, Mp 14.9. CGCG – Anon., Mp 14.9. POSS – plate O–672, v. compact core in e.f., diffuse, circular envelope.

A 058	MCG 9–17–9	09 57.8 +55 57	16½-inch

Observation: lies 40 sec. of R.A. p. and 2 arc-min N. of NGC 3079. Best seen at x176 and x351 when it appears to be small, faint and sl.el. E–W. Of uniform surface brightness.
References: MCG – 9–17–9, (N), Mp 15.0. UGC – in Notes for NGC 3079 but incorrectly listed as N.f. instead of N.p. CGCG – Anon., Mp 14.6. POSS – plate O–1331, small, sl.el. N.p.–S.f., uniform surface brightness except for bright spot towards f. end.

A 059	MCG 9–17–11	09 59.1 +54 06	16½-inch

Observation: detected at x176. Faint, medium size and el. E–W. It is of uniform surface brightness with only a hint of a central brightening; seems quite narrow. Lies between 2 widely separated stars with a faint star close N.p.
References: MCG – 9–17–11, (Nn), Ra, Mp 15.0. UGC & CGCG – not listed. POSS – plate O–1331.

A 060	RNGC 3099B	09 59.6 +32 56	16½-inch

Observation: lies 9 sec. of R.A. p. and on the same Dec. as NGC 3099. It is a small compact nebulous knot. Very faint and of uniform surface brightness. Best seen with a.v.
References: MCG – lists an object 3 sec. of R.A. p. and 1 arc-min N. of NGC 3099. Mp 14.9. UGC & CGCG – not listed. RNGC – listed as RNGC 3099B, Mp 16.0. POSS – plate O–1345, compact, stellar nucleus with a small envelope.

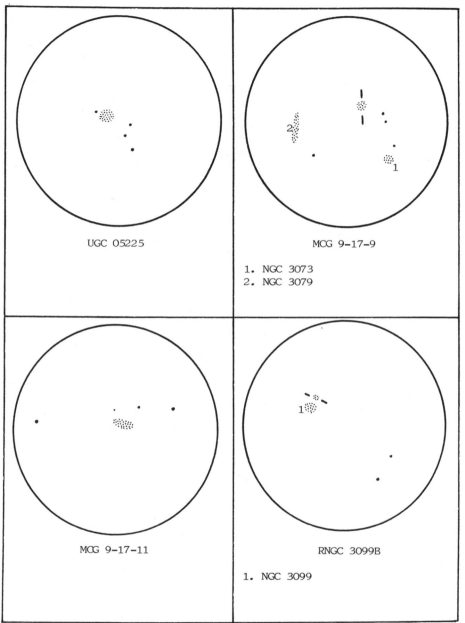

UGC 05225

MCG 9-17-9

1. NGC 3073
2. NGC 3079

MCG 9-17-11

RNGC 3099B

1. NGC 3099

W.S. No.	Name	R.A. (1950) Dec.	Telescope

A 061   UGC 05435   10 02.5   +59 03   16½-inch

Observation: quite bright but v. compact, alm. stell., requiring x176 to suggest a nebular image. More clearly non-stellar at x351 but no other details visible. Lies within a triangle of 3 stars of similar mag. Coarse dbl. lies S.f., comp's S.p.-N.f. **References:** MCG - 10-15-13, (E?), Mp 15.0. UGC - 05435, 0'.8 x 0'.4, Mp 13.6. CGCG - Anon., Mp 13.6. POSS - plate O-962, compact image slightly extended S.p.-N.f.

A 062   UGC 05451   10 04.2   +47 16   16½-inch

Observation: easily visible at x84; small, faint, irregularly round, brightens considerably to the centre to a v. small nuc. 2 stars of similar mag. preceding, aligned almost N-S. **References:** MCG - 8-19-4, (N), Isb, 1ℓba, Mp 14.0. UGC - 05451, 1'.6 x 0'.8, Irr., Mp 14.1. CGCG - Anon., Mp 14.1. POSS - plate O-1348.

A 063   UGC 05459   10 04.9   +53 19   16½-inch

Observation: v. well seen at x176, appearing as a surprisingly bright, greatly elongated streak, extended N.p.-S.f. Wider and brighter towards the f. end while p. end narrows to a point. It lies close to a brighter star which, with 3 others, forms a greatly elongated diamond aligned N.p.-S.f. **References:** MCG - 9-17-27, Fc, Mp 12.0. UGC - 05459, 4'.3 x 0'.5, Sc, P.A. 132°, Mp 13.8. CGCG - Anon., Mp 13.8. POSS - plate O-1331, bright, v. el., star at N.tip of f. extension, p. end diff.

A 064   UGC 05475   10 06.1   +58 42   16½-inch

Observation: at x84, very faint and very compact. Lies close S.p. a faint star with a much brighter star at a distance N. At x176, seen as a small round image with a brighter nucleus. **References:** MCG - 10-15-19, B, 2Sa, Hb, Mp 15.0. UGC - 05475, 1'.7 x 0'.8, SBc, P.A. 38°, Mp 15.5. CGCG - Anon., Mp 15.5. POSS - plate O-962, v. diff. object extended S.p.-N.f., brighter central lens with a faint envelope surrounding.

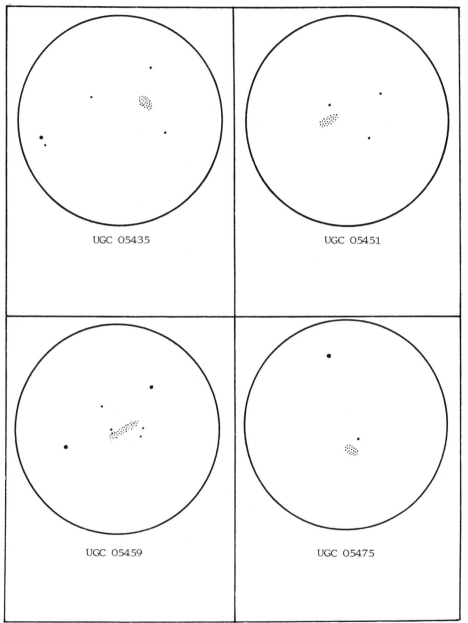

UGC 05435

UGC 05451

UGC 05459

UGC 05475

W.S. No.	Name	R.A.	(1950)	Dec.	Telescope

A 065   Unlisted   10 10.5   +38 53   16½-inch

Observation: lies 14 sec. of R.A. p. and 8 arc-min S. of NGC 3158,
appearing as a very small, very faint nebular image f. NGC 3151.
At the same place there was a very faint star with the flickering
nebular image beside it. Nebula very difficult to confirm.
References: MCG, UGC & CGCG - not listed. POSS - plate O-711,
compact, having a v. sm. env. with a developed lens. Greatest
part of envelope is located on S. end of central lens.

A 066   Unlisted   10 10.6   +38 59   16½-inch

Observation: lies 11 sec. of R.A. p. and 2 arc-min S. of NGC 3158,
directly N. of a star S.p. NGC 3158. First noticed with x351 as a
very faint, small knot. Also seen at x422. Star S. acts as a
good comparison to confirm its nebular identity.
References: MCG, UGC & CGCG - not listed. POSS - plate O-711,
stellar in appearance. Very slightly extended N-S. Very compact
with no visible envelope.

A 067   MCG 7-21-19   10 10.7   +38 55   16½-inch

Observation: lies 6 sec. of R.A. p. and 6 arc-min S. of NGC 3158.
Extremely faint, pretty large, oval and of uniform surface
brightness. Lies N.p. NGC 3159.
References: MCG - 7-21-19, B+2e, Mp 15.0. UGC & CGCG - not
listed. POSS - plate O-711, small, sl. el. almost E-W. Envelope
easily distinguished; bright central lens sl. el. S.p.-N.f.

A 068   MCG 7-21-34   10 12.8   +44 02   16½-inch

Observation: extremely faint and very difficult. It is of uniform
surface brightness and at times there is the impression of an e.f.
star off S. end. Faint star pretty close p. while at a similar
separation f. there is a slightly brighter one. Another star S.
References: MCG - 7-21-34, F;H, Mp 16.0. UGC - not listed.
CGCG - Anon., Mp 14.7. POSS - plate O-711, appears much as
described, irregular in shape with its small image el. N-S.

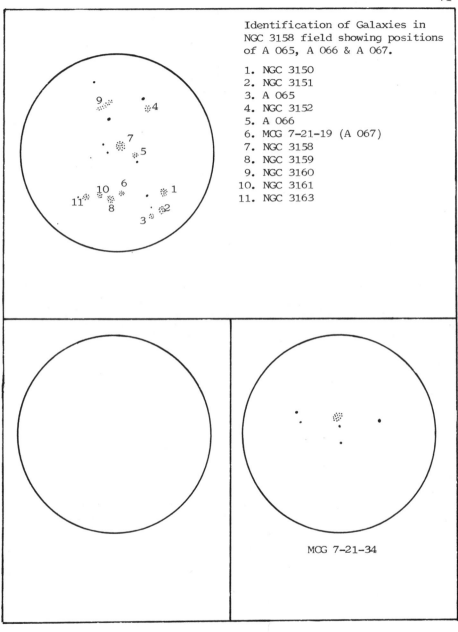

Identification of Galaxies in
NGC 3158 field showing positions
of A 065, A 066 & A 067.

1. NGC 3150
2. NGC 3151
3. A 065
4. NGC 3152
5. A 066
6. MCG 7-21-19 (A 067)
7. NGC 3158
8. NGC 3159
9. NGC 3160
10. NGC 3161
11. NGC 3163

MCG 7-21-34

W.S. No.	Name	R.A. (1950) Dec.		Telescope

A 069   UGC 05542   10 13.5   +60 32   16½-inch

Observation: lies 20 sec. of R.A. f. and 3 arc-min N. of NGC 3168.
Suspected at x84 but required x176 to confirm. Small; brightens
to a stellar nucleus, surrounded by a small envelope. It lies
about 2/3 distance separating NGC 3168 from first bright star S.
References: MCG – 10-15-54, E, Mp 14.0. UGC – 05542, 1'.0 x 1'.0,
Compact, Mp 14.9. CGCG – Anon., Compact, Mp 14.9. POSS – plate
0-962, compact, very small circular envelope.

A 070   MCG 4-25-4   10 18.2   +25 46   16½-inch

Observation: lies 20 sec. of R.A. f. and 1 arc-min N. of NGC 3209.
Irregularly round, quite faint but easily confirmed at x351. Very
bright star directly N. at a distance.
References: MCG – 4-25-4, (Ne)?, Mp 15.2. UGC – in Notes as comp.
to NGC 3209. CGCG – Anon., Mp 15.2. POSS – plate 0-1380, compact
with extremely small env., I was able to detect the extended
nucleus questioned by Vorontsov-Velyaminov in the MCG.

A 071   MCG 10-15-70   10 19.2   +57 17   16½-inch

Observation: lies 36 sec of R.A. p. and 1 arc-min S. of NGC 3214.
Longer but fainter than NGC 3214; irregularly round and of uniform
surface brightness. A star lies close S.
References: MCG – 10-15-70, (Np), (b)+*, Mp 15.0. UGC – not
listed. CGCG – Anon., Mp 15.6. POSS – plate 0-962, nucleus sl.
el. N.p.-S.f., as is the envelope. Longer than NGC 3214, f. end
slightly wider than p. end.

A 072   MCG 7-21-47   10 19.2   +38 45   16½-inch

Observation: lies 30 sec. of R.A. p. and 4 arc-min S. of NGC 3219.
Quite large, irregular, uniform surface brightness, may be sl. el.
almost N-S. May be brighter than NGC 3219. Lies close N.f. the
bright star which is S.p. NGC 3219.
References: MCG – 7-21-47 & 48, dbl. system, E+E, Mp 14.7. UGC –
not listed. CGCG – lists NGC 3219 as a dbl. system. POSS – plate
0-711, unusual appearance with a 'double nucleus' in a halo of
nebulosity extended almost N-S.

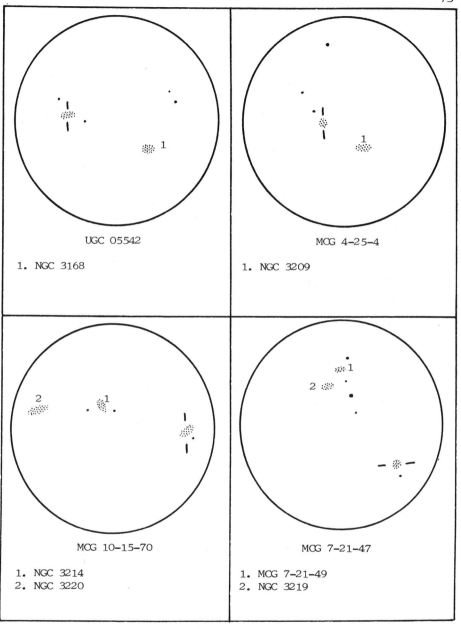

UGC 05542

1. NGC 3168

MCG 4-25-4

1. NGC 3209

MCG 10-15-70

1. NGC 3214
2. NGC 3220

MCG 7-21-47

1. MCG 7-21-49
2. NGC 3219

74

A 073   MCG 7-21-49   10 19.5   +38 50 $16\frac{1}{2}$-inch

Observation: lies 11 sec. of R.A. p. and 1 arc-min N. of NGC 3219.
Faint, v. small, appearing only as a small nebulous knot of
uniformly bright nebulosity. Best seen with x351.
References: MCG - 7-21-49, Nn, Lb, Mp 14.7. UGC & CGCG - not
listed. POSS - plate O-711, small and faint. Small stellar nuc.
with a diffuse env. consisting of elongated wings N.p.-S.f.

A 074   UGC 05602   10 19.6   +22 41 $16\frac{1}{2}$-inch

Observation: extremely faint, small and appears to be elongated
N.p.-S.f. Star just off S. end. With x427, seen as a small ray
or streak of nebulosity of uniform surface brightness.
References: MCG - not listed. UGC - 05602, 1'.1 x 0'.5, SB7,
P.A. 128°, Mp 16.0. CGCG - not listed. POSS - plate O-1380,
very small, elongated, N.p. extension longer than S.f.

A 075   MCG 3-27-12   10 20.0   +19 41 $17\frac{1}{2}$-inch*

Observation: round with a much brighter core, not difficult with
direct vision at x94. Star on S.p. edge, beyond outer envelope.
References: MCG - 3-27-12, F;H, Mp 15.4. UGC - not listed.
CGCG - Anon., Mp 15.4. POSS - plate O-58, very small, little
extended N.p.-S.f. Round bright core with a faint envelope.

A 076   UGC 05622   10 20.8   +34 01   13.1-inch*

Observation: at x187 it is very faint, but distinctly seen with
a.v. It has a brighter condensed nucleus surrounded by a round,
diffuse envelope. With good seeing and dark adaption it can be
seen with direct vision.
References: MCG - 6-23-11, n, 2B, 1sb, 1 shop→c;H, Mp 14.0.
UGC - 05622, 1'.3 x 0'.9, Sb/SBc, Mp 15.4. CGCG - Anon., ZWG
183.020, Mp 15.4. POSS - plate O-1032, very small, round and
faint. Brightens in the middle, diffuse outer envelope.

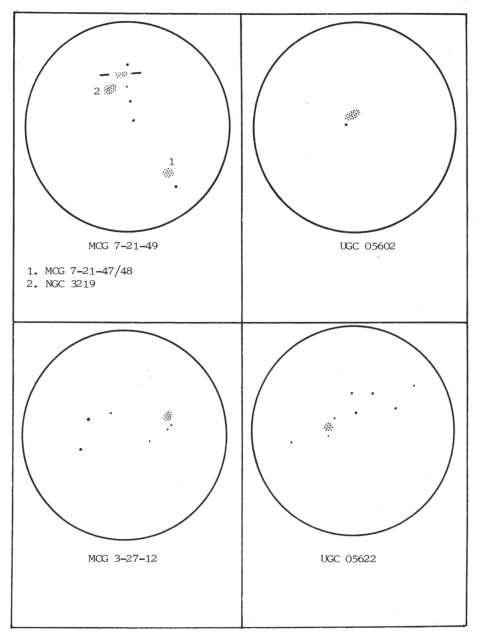

MCG 7-21-49

1. MCG 7-21-47/48
2. NGC 3219

UGC 05602

MCG 3-27-12

UGC 05622

W.S. No.	Name	R.A. (1950) Dec.	Telescope
A 077	UGC 05662	10 24.2 +28 54	16½-inch

Observation: lies 18 sec. of R.A. p. and 8 arc-min N. of NGC 3245.
First seen with x176. It is v. faint, quite large, elongated
N.p.-S.f. and of uniform surface brightness. 2 stars of equal
mag. lie close N., aligned S.p.-N.f.; galaxy points at S. star.
References: MCG - 5-25-12, L, 2faf, Mp 15.4. UGC - 05662, 3'.6 x
0'.3, SBb, P.A. 150°, Mp 15.4. CGCG - Anon., Mp 15.4. POSS -
0-1387, long, narrow edge-on with extended central area and
compact nucleus.

A 078	UGC 05672	10 25.6 +22 50	16½-inch

Observation: small and faint but not difficult at x84. At x176,
irregular and somewhat extended N.p.-S.f. E.f. star close to S.
end seen at x351. Trapezium of stars p., another star directly S.
References: MCG - 4-25-21, F;H, Mp 14.9. UGC - 05672, 2'.3 x
0'.6, S, P.A. 158°, Mp 14.9. CGCG - Anon., Mp 14.9. POSS - plate
0-1380, elongated image with very diffuse extensions.

A 079	UGC 05679	10 26.1 +26 36	16½-inch

Observation: N. of 3 galaxies in field; 36 sec. of R.A. p. and 15
arc-min N. of NGC 3251 (=IC 2579). Best seen at x176 when it
appears small, faint, of uniform surface brightness and possibly
slightly extended N.p.-S.f. Fairly bright star S.p.
References: MCG - 5-25-15, N, 2?a, Mp 15.4. UGC - 05679, 1'.7 x
0'.6, S, P.A. 122°, Mp 15.4. CGCG - Anon., Mp 15.4. POSS - plate
0-1387, extended almost E-W, extensions very weak, stell. nuc.

A 080	Unlisted	10 26.6 +26 20	16½-inch

Observation: lies 8 sec. of R.A. f. and 1 arc-min S. of NGC 3251.
Seen as a very small, very faint nebulous image close S.f. NGC
3251. No other details apparent.
References: MCG & CGCG - not listed. UGC - in Notes as comp. to
UGC 05684, 2'.1 distant, P.A. 140°, 0'.55 x 0'.15. POSS - plate
0-1380, very small, faint elongated system, brighter in central
area. Major axis aligned N.f.-S.P.

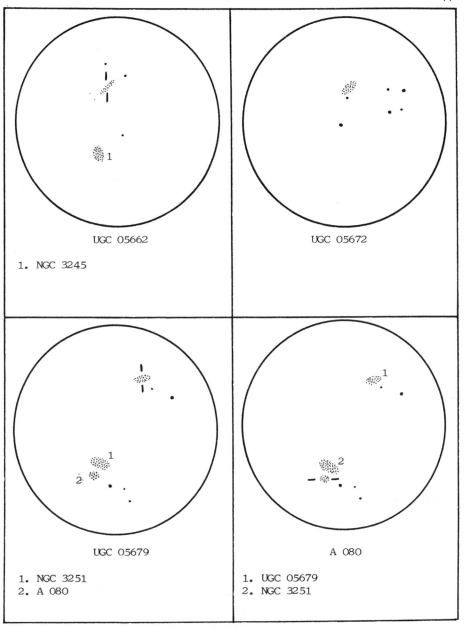

UGC 05662

1. NGC 3245

UGC 05672

UGC 05679

1. NGC 3251
2. A 080

A 080

1. UGC 05679
2. NGC 3251

W.S. No.	Name	R.A. (1950) Dec.	Telescope

A 081   UGC 05791   10 36.5   +48 12   16½-inch

Observation: first seen with x176; very faint, irregular and of
uniform surface brightness. May be extended S.p.-N.f. Faint
star close N.f. which in turn has a fainter star S.f.
References: MCG - 8-20-004, (N), 1sb, 1 pa, Mp 14.0. UGC - 05791,
1'.6 x 0'.5, P.A. 43°, Mp 14.4. CGCG - Anon., Mp 14.4. POSS -
plate 0-709, small elongated system, extended S.p.-N.f. Uniform
surface brightness. Slight curve in N.f. extension.

A 082   UGC 05798   10 36.8   +48 11   16½-inch

Observation: lies S.f. UGC 05791 (A 081). It is small, faint and
a little extended S.p.-N.f. It is S.p. the more distant star f.
UGC 05791.
References: MCG - 8-20-11, F, Mp 14.0. UGC - 05798, 1'.0 x 0'.22,
P.A. 45°, Mp 14.5. CGCG - Anon., Mp 14.5. POSS - plate 0-709,
extended system, slightly wider on N.f. end, brighter than A 081.

A 083   UGC 05838   10 40.5   +41 03   16½-inch

Observation: easily visible at x84. Small, sl.el. N.p.-S.f.;
medium size, brightens in the centre with narrow extensions.
Faint star close p. Better seen at x176 when nucleus is small and
bright; star p. has fainter comp. f. and there is an e.f. star
just off p. extension. At x351 p. extension is brighter than f.
References: MCG - 7-22-48, Ne, 2⊘d→8, 1⊘fc, Mp 14.0. UGC -
05838, 1'.3 x 0'.5, SBb, P.A. 130°, Mp 14.0. CGCG - Anon., Mp
14.0. POSS - plate 0-690, quite br. el. system, small nuc. a
little extended E-W, outer env. contained in a dark ring.

A 084   UGC 05839   10 40.6   +39 57   16½-inch

Observation: small, faint, elongated, more narrow than A 083.
Brightens in centre to small nuc. Well seen at x351, when it is
wider and brighter in middle; extensions easily visible. Faint
stars noted directly N. and S.p.
References: MCG - 7-22-49, (Ne), H, Mp 15.0. UGC - 05839, 1'.2 x
0'.3, SO-a, P.A. 146°, Mp 14.8. CGCG - Anon., Mp 14.2. POSS -
plate 0-690, oval shaped with faint outer extensions, more
prominent on N.p. end. Elongated as described.

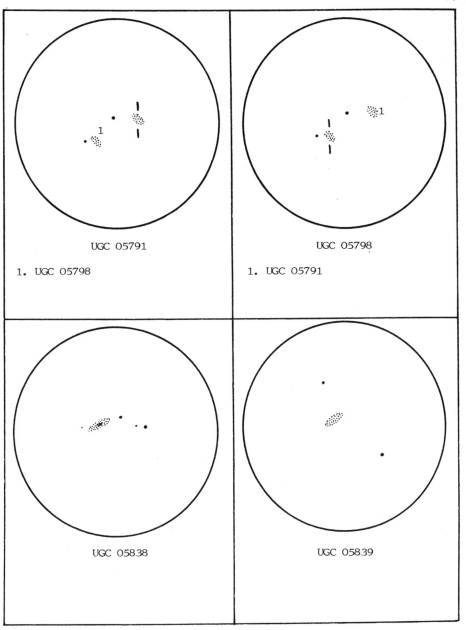

UGC 05791

1. UGC 05798

UGC 05798

1. UGC 05791

UGC 05838

UGC 05839

W.S. No.	Name	R.A. (1950) Dec.		Telescope
A 085	UGC 05903	10 45.2	+28 31	13.1-inch*

Observation: first noticed with x94 and confirmed with x147 when it appeared as a very faint, round patch, of uniform brightness. **References:** MCG – 5-26-11, N, 2B →2sm→8, H, Mp 15.1. UGC – 05903, SBa-b, 1'.1 x 0'.7, Mp 15.1. CGCG – Anon., ZWG 155.014, Mp 15.1. POSS – plate O-1357, small, slightly extended S.p.-N.f. Uniformly bright.

A 086	UGC 05958	10 48.5	+28 07	13.1-inch*

Observation: v. difficult, seen only with a.v. during good seeing. A little extended N-S, uniform surface brightness. **References:** MCG – 5-26-22, Fb, Mp 15.6. UGC – 05958, 1'.6 x 0'.3, Sb-c, P.A. 179°, Mp 15.6. CGCG – Anon., ZWG 155.028, Mp 15.6. POSS – small, very thin edge-on, extended N-S, uniformly bright.

A 087	UGC 06112	10 59.9	+17 00	16½-inch

Observation: extremely faint, diffuse, v. difficult with x84. Quite long and elongated N.p.-S.f. Still barely visible with x176 when it appears quite wide, long and of uniform surface brightness. **References:** MCG – 3-28-50, L, 2ℓₐ, H, Mp 14.5. UGC – 06112, 2'.3 x 0'.8, Sc-✕meg., P.A. 123°, Mp 14.5. CGCG – Anon., Mp 14.5. POSS – plate O-463, very much extended with long, bright, narrow central area surrounded by a very diffuse envelope.

A 088	UGC 06276	11 12.4	+31 18	17½-inch*

Observation: x167 shows it to be bright, round, brighter towards the middle with a possibly compact nucleus. Slightly smaller than nearby UGC 06367 (A 090). **References:** MCG – 5-27-32, E?, Mp 14.4. UGC – 06276, S0, Mp 14.4. CGCG – Anon., ZWG 156.036, Mp 14.4. POSS – plate O-99, small, round, brighter core surrounded by a faint, thin round outer envelope. Smaller than UGC 06367.

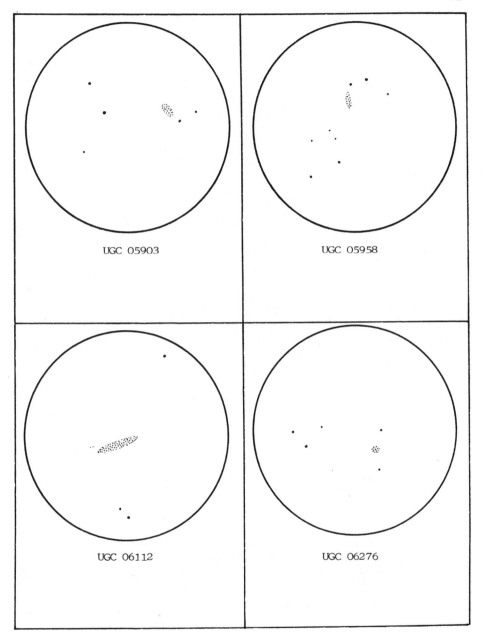

UGC 05903

UGC 05958

UGC 06112

UGC 06276

W.S. No.	Name	R.A. (1950) Dec.	Telescope

A 089 UGC 06355   11 18.0   +31 30   17½-inch*

Observation: at x167 appears to be very extended, thin and of
even brightness. The edges are definite but not sharp. Star
near p. tip. UGC 06367 (A 090) lies in the same field.
References: MCG – +05–27–059, Fc, Mp 14.8. UGC – 06355, Sc,
Mp 14.8. CGCG – Anon., ZWG 156.065, Mp 14.8. POSS – plate 0–99,
very much extended E–W, thin edge-on, gradually brighter in the
middle, with obvious star just off p. tip.

A 090 UGC 06367   11 18.4   +31 31   17½-inch*

Observation: at x167 appears slightly brighter than UGC 06355,
and about half the size or slightly smaller. Round and of
uniform surface brightness.
References: MCG – +05–27–060, N;Dab, Mp 15.0. UGC – 06367,
SBa–b, Mp 15.0. CGCG – Anon., ZWG 156.066, Mp 15.0. POSS –
plate 0–99, small, slightly extended core area (N.p.–S.f.), in a
round, thin outer envelope. Core off set to S. edge of envelope.

A 091 UGC 06527   11 29.9   +53 14   16½-inch

Observation: lies about 7 arc-min S. of NGC 3718, and is really a
group of connected galaxies. Visible at x84 but better seen at
x176; v. narrow, el. S.p.–N.f., uniformly bright except for br.
patch on f. end. At x351, darker region in central area, p. part
brighter, f. end brightens to small, almost stellar region.
References: MCG – 9–19–111, (N)+(Np)+(Np)+Fp, Mp 15.0. UGC –
06527, 1'.1 x 0'.6, connected triple system, Mp 14.7. CGCG –
Anon., quintuple system, Mp 14.7. POSS – plate 0–059, curved
line of connected galaxies, br. on f. end. Edge-on close S.f.

A 092 UGC 06534   11 30.4   +63 34   16½-inch

Observation: easy with x84 and well seen with x176; narrow, but
broader in centre. Central brightening extended along maj. axis.
References: MCG – 11–14–30, F, Mp 14.0. UGC – 06534, 3'.0 x
0'.8, Sc, P.A. 60°, Mp 13.3. CGCG – Anon., Mp 13.3. POSS –
central area extended, no nuc. evident, p. end very diffuse.

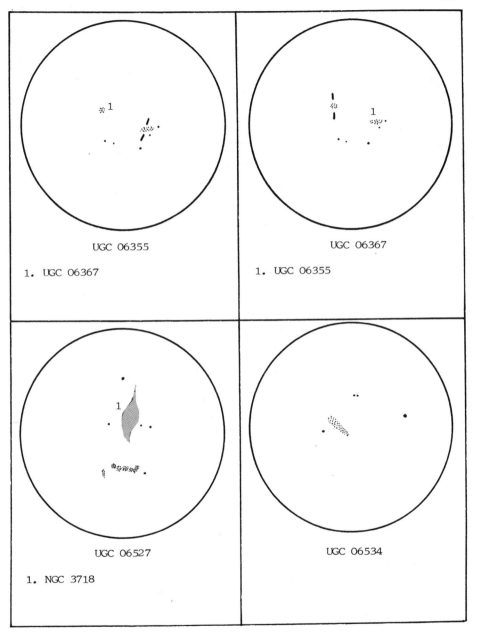

UGC 06355

1. UGC 06367

UGC 06367

1. UGC 06355

UGC 06527

1. NGC 3718

UGC 06534

W.S. No.	Name	R.A. (1950) Dec.		Telescope

A 093   UGC 06552   11 31.5   +71 49   16½-inch

Observation: susp. at x84 but easily verified at x176. It is
extremely small and faint, elongated S.p.-N.f. and uniformly
br. Perhaps wider on p. end. Lies S.f. a faint star.
References: MCG - 12-11-34, Fc, Mp 15.0. UGC - 06552, 1'.2 x
0'.45, S, P.A. 46°, Mp 14.3. CGCG - Anon., Mp 14.3. POSS -
plate 0-714, small 'hook' or arm on N. side of p. end. Shows a
small central brightening.

A 094   MCG 9-19-125   11 32.2   +54 55   16½-inch

Observation: p., faintest and smallest of 3 galaxies in the same
field; lies 48 sec. of R.A. and 8 arc-min N. of NGC 3738. It is
faint, round and uniformly bright at x84, though central area
brightens a little at x176. Coarse double lies S.p.
References: MCG - 9-19-125, L, SSct, Mp 15.0. UGC - not listed.
CGCG - Anon., Mp 14.9. POSS - plate 0-59, bright nucleus in a
circular lens, with a tight spiral arm on f. side. Faint star or
knot invested in N.p. edge.

A 095   UGC 06582   11 34.2   +55 26   16½-inch

Observation: easily visible at x84; medium size, oval, slightly
brighter centre. At x176, faint star seen just off N.f. edge.
Bright star close N.p. while at a slightly greater distance is an
'arrowhead' group of 4 stars. Nucleus stellar at x351.
References: MCG - 9-19-135, N, ɣc→R?, Mp 14.0. UGC - 06582, 1'.4
x 1'.2, SBb-c, Mp 14.5. CGCG - Anon., Mp 14.5. POSS - plate 0-
59, round spiral with prominent arm N. Bright lens with stellar
nucleus. Envelope of greater extent on f. side.

A 096   UGC 06604   11 35.4   +59 02   16½-inch

Observation: easy at x84; small, oval, with an envelope of uniform
brightness around a bright stell.nuc. Best seen with x176 when
nucleus is very evident. Lies in field of 3 widely spaced stars.
References: MCG - 10-17-29, E, Mp 14.0. UGC - 06604, 1'.0 x 1'.0,
Type ?, Mp 14.0. CGCG - Anon., Mp 14.0. POSS - plate 0-723, sm.,
round, bright lens with v. small diffuse envelope. Elliptical ?

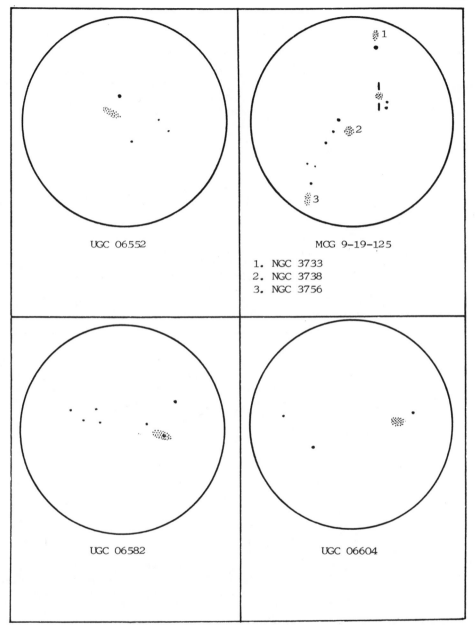

UGC 06552

MCG 9-19-125

1. NGC 3733
2. NGC 3738
3. NGC 3756

UGC 06582

UGC 06604

W.S. No.	Name	R.A. (1950) Dec.		Telescope

A 097   UGC 06616   11 36.6   +58 33   16½-inch

Observation: quite easy although faint and diffuse. Medium size
and somewhat irregular in shape. Resembles a faint PN. At x176,
faint star close to N.f. edge. At a distance S.f. there is a
very bright star which has a double just N.p. V.f. star just S.
References: MCG - 10-17-35, L, 2scm;4sb, Db, Mp 14.0. UGC -
06616, 3'.0 x 2'.4, Sc, Mp 14.2. CGCG - Anon., Mp 14.2. POSS -
plate 0-723, irregularly shaped galaxy with knotty central area,
offset to N. edge of env. Star superimposed on S. edge.

A 098   UGC 06658   11 39.4   +32 17   13.1-inch*

Observation: a difficult object, seen only with a.v. at x94. V.f.
patch of nebulosity, slightly elliptical and of uniform surface
brightness, a little extended N.p.-S.f. Barely visible at x147.
References: MCG - 5-28-16, F, 1Sb, Mp 15.4. UGC - 06658, 1'.0 x
0'.4, S, P.A. 129°, Mp 15.0. CGCG - Anon., ZWG 157.016, Mp 15.0.
POSS - plate 0-1379, small sl.el. N.p.-S.f. Uniformly bright.

A 099   UGC 06666   11 39.7   +16 18   16½-inch

Observation: easily visible at x84; small, faint and of uniform
surface brightness. No additional details noted at x176 & x427.
No nucleus noted. Lies f. 2 stars aligned S.p.-N.f. with a
brighter star in line with and N.f. these.
References: MCG - 3-30-50, F?, Mp 14.3. UGC - 06666, 1'.1 x 1'.4,
S, Mp 14.3. CGCG - Anon., Mp 14.3. POSS - plate 0-1406, small
galaxy with a developed nucleus and small extensions N & S. Most
of nebular structure appears N. of the nucleus.

A 100   UGC 06670   11 39.8   +18 36   13.1-inch*

Observation: easily visible at x147 as an extended object of
even brightness. Major axis aligned almost N-S with N extension
the brighter.
References: MCG - 3-30-53, F, Mp 14.3. UGC - 06670, 3'.1 x 0'.9,
Irregular, P.A. 153°, Mp 14.3. CGCG - Anon., ZWG 97.067, Mp 14.3.
POSS - plate 0-1406, very much extended N.p.-S.f. Bright image,
extended bright nuc. in obviously elongated envelope.

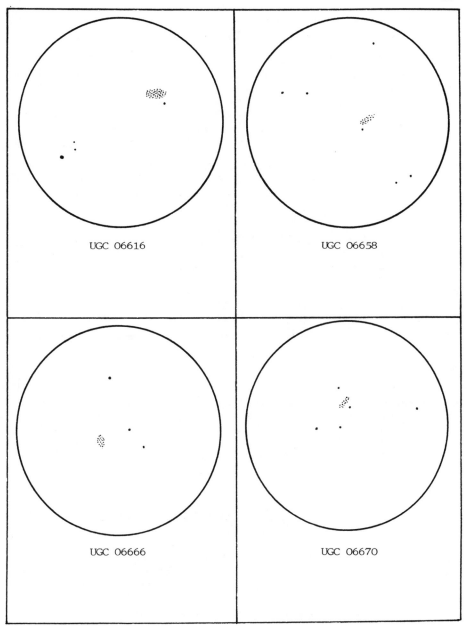

UGC 06616

UGC 06658

UGC 06666

UGC 06670

W.S. No.	Name	R.A. (1950) Dec.	Telescope
A 101	MCG 3-30-51	11 39.8 +20 24	16½-inch

Observation: lies 36 sec. of R.A. f. and 1 arc-min N. of NGC 3816 and between 2 stars aligned almost N-S. At x176 it is quite small, irregularly round and brightens in the middle.
References: MCG - 3-30-51, Ne, ꙮ pa, Mp 14.7. UGC - in Notes re. NGC 3816, 0'.9 x 0'.7, S, Mp 14.7. CGCG - Anon., Mp 14.7. POSS - plate O-1406, small, bright central area with diffuse 'wings' N.p.-S.f. Easily visible between the two stars described.

A 102	UGC 06697	11 41.2 +20 15	13.1-inch*

Observation: lies 12 sec. of R.A. p. and 2 arc-min N. of NGC 3842. It is faint, of uniform surface brightness, quite narrow and elongated N.p.-S.f. Faint star between it and NGC 3842.
References: MCG - 3-30-66, FC, Mp 14.3. UGC - 06697, 1'.7 x 0'.3, Irr., P.A. 137°, Mp 14.3. CGCG - Anon., Mp 14.3. RNGC - peculiar object p. NGC 3842. POSS - plate O-1406, narrow streak of nebulosity, brighter at S.f. end which also curves slightly S.

A 103	UGC 06719	11 42.2 +20 24	16½-inch

Observation: lies 48 sec. of R.A. f. and 11 arc-min N. of NGC 3842. It is faint, quite long and diffuse. Brightens on S.p. edge. N.f. are 3 stars in line N.p.-S.f.
References: MCG - 3-30-89, L, 1 8, H, Mp 14.6. UGC - 06719, 1'.2 x 0'.8, S, P.A. 30°, Mp 14.6. CGCG - Anon., Mp 14.6. POSS - plate O-1406, small, compact galaxy. Br. nuc. with small env., most extensive on N. edge. Small curving arm on S. edge.

A 104	UGC 06753	11 44.2 +14 49	17½-inch*

Observation: not visible at x94. Seen at x147 with good dark adaption as elliptical, el. E-W, and gradually brighter to the middle. Very diffuse, ill-defined. Star just off N.p. edge.
References: MCG - 3-30-110, F, 1 bc, 1 w, Mp 15.5. UGC - 06753, 1'.1 x 0'.6, SB, P.A. 90°, Mp 15.3. CGCG - Anon., ZWG 097.146, Mp 15.3. POSS - plate O-1406, small, slightly extended E-W, brighter core with fainter, elongated outer envelope.

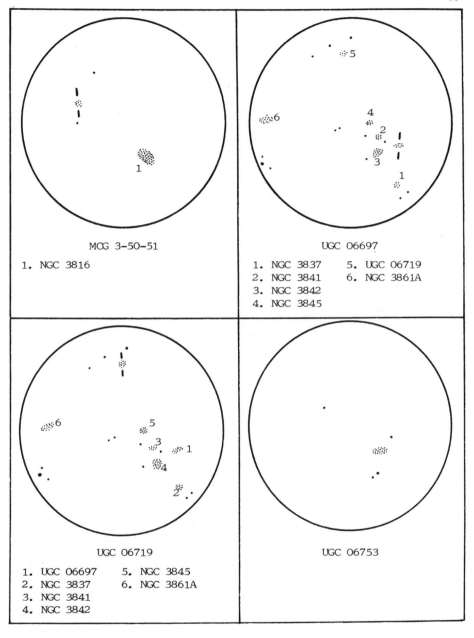

MCG 3-50-51

1. NGC 3816

UGC 06697

1. NGC 3837	5. UGC 06719
2. NGC 3841	6. NGC 3861A
3. NGC 3842	
4. NGC 3845	

UGC 06719

1. UGC 06697	5. NGC 3845
2. NGC 3837	6. NGC 3861A
3. NGC 3841	
4. NGC 3842	

UGC 06753

W.S. No.	Name	R.A. (1950) Dec.		Telescope
A 105	MCG 9-19-191	11 45.2	+56 16	16½-inch

Observation: lies 18 sec. of R.A. f. and 2 arc-min N. of NGC 3888, between this and the most southerly of 3 stars in line which are N.f. It is small, very faint and compact.
References: MCG - 9-19-191, N; H, Mp 16.0. UGC - in Notes as companion to NGC 3888, 0'.5 x 0'.4. CGCG - not listed. POSS - plate 0-59, stellar, compact, envelope almost non-existent.

A 106	MCG 6-26-43	11 48.8	+35 30	17½-inch*

Observation: easily seen at x94, within a triangle of obvious stars. Very diffuse, slightly elliptical and has a small stell. nuc. which appears to be offset towards f. end.
References: MCG 6-26-43, N; H, Mp 16.0. UGC - not listed. CGCG Anon., ZWG 186.056, Mp 15.6. POSS - plate 0-109, very small, round image. V.f. diffuse outer envelope with brighter centre.

A 107	CGCG Anon.	12 05.3	+67 40	16½-inch

Observation: lies 66 sec. of R.A. f. and 14 arc-min N. of NGC 4108 but should not be confused with either 4108A or 4108B. It is the 4th galaxy visible in the field and lies N. of NGC 4108B. It is brighter than 4108B and is of irregular shape.
References: MCG & UGC - not listed. CGCG - Anon., Mp 14.7. POSS - plate 0-674, easily visible as a small, round object with a developed central lens in a small envelope.

A 108	UGC 07287	12 13.7	+28 25	16½-inch

Observation: located 36 sec. of R.A. f. and 2 arc-min S. of NGC 4211, and directly N. of a bright star f. NGC 4211. Easily identified at x176, irregular, uniform surface brightness.
References: MCG - 5-29-46, n, 2Bw, 2ℰbzo, Db, Mp 15.5. UGC - 07287, 1'.1 x 0'.7, SBc, P.A. 75°, Mp 15.5. CGCG - Anon., Mp 15.5. POSS - plate 0-1398, small, faint, barred spiral? Ovaloid in shape with stell. nuc. Major axis aligned almost E-W.

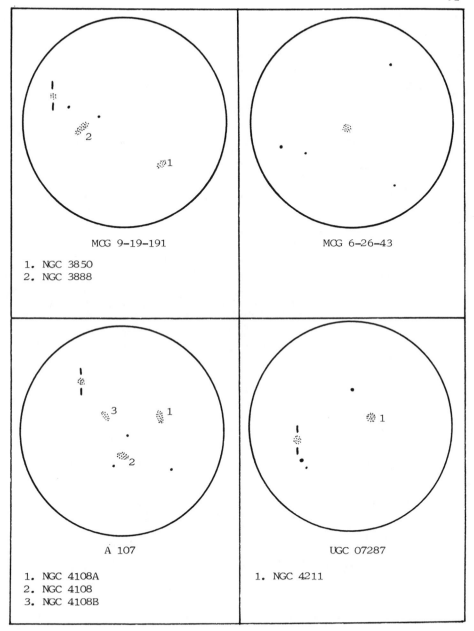

MCG 9-19-191

1. NGC 3850
2. NGC 3888

MCG 6-26-43

A 107

1. NGC 4108A
2. NGC 4108
3. NGC 4108B

UGC 07287

1. NGC 4211

W.S. No.	Name	R.A. (1950) Dec.	Telescope
A 109	UGC 07593	12 25.8 +44 43	16½-inch

Observation: v.f. but visible at x84, p. a small triangle of
stars, 2 closest aligned N.p.-S.f. while the 3rd and brightest
lies S. The galaxy is small, of uniform surface brightness and
possibly extended N.p.-S.f. At x351 another nebular image susp.,
very close N.p., or it may be an extremely faint star.
References: MCG - 8-23-38 & 39, N; 12 and N; 12 wb., Mp 16.0 &
16.0. UGC - 07593, 1'.2 x 0'.9, Dbl. system connected, Mp 14.8.
CGCG - not listed. POSS - plate O-1408, extended E-W with curved
appendage coming off f. end under the major axis while a diffuse
area lies above p. end and has a faint star superimposed.

A 110	Unlisted	12 48.7 +47 58	16½-inch

Observation: has same R.A. and is 2 arc-min N. of NGC 4741. First
noted at x176 as faint knot close p. the N. end of NGC 4741; very
difficult to confirm as a nebular image due to its faintness.
References: MCG, UGC & CGCG - not listed. POSS - plate O-1350,
sl. el. E-W, uniform surface brightness, elliptical.

A 111	UGC 08015	12 50.4 +10 16	16½-inch

Observation: v.f. but found with x84, close N. of 2 stars of
similar mag. aligned N.p.-S.f. Better seen with x176; irregular
in shape, medium size, little sign of any central brightening.
References: MCG - 2-33-32, L?, D; 1 sta., Mp 15.1. UGC - 08015,
1'.8 x 1'.1, Sa-b, P.A. 60°, Mp 15.1. CGCG - Anon., Mp 15.1.
POSS - plate O-041, beautiful spiral, stell. nuc., longer lens
with spiral arms almost completely surrounding the envelope.

A 112	UGC 08032	12 52.2 +13 30	16½-inch

Observation: visible at x84. Very narrow, major axis slightly
N.p.-S.f.; brightens only slightly in the middle. Star p. tip of
S. extension with a much fainter star close f.
References: MCG - 2-33-35, F; Mp 14.8. UGC - 08032, 2'.7 x 0'.6,
S, P.A. 167°, Mp 14.8. CGCG - Anon., Mp 14.8. POSS - plate O-
041, highly inclined system with bright central area, no nucleus
visible. Greatly extended.

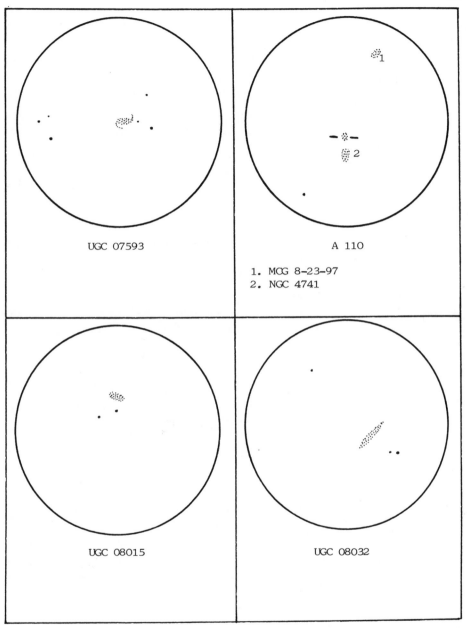

UGC 07593

A 110

1. MCG 8-23-97
2. NGC 4741

UGC 08015

UGC 08032

W.S. No.	Name	R.A. (1950) Dec.		Telescope
A 113	MCG 9-21-62	12 54.2	+52 24	16½-inch

Observation: lies 66 sec. of R.A. p. and 2 arc-min. S. of NGC 4834. It is extremely faint, medium size and diffuse, with no central brightening. Star close p. has fainter companion N. and slightly f.
References: MCG - 9-21-62, N; (2B-), Reb, 2Sfc, Mp 14.0. UGC - not listed. CGCG - Anon., Mp 15.5. POSS - plate O-729, diffuse spiral with 2 main arms. Stellar nucleus.

A 114	Unlisted	12 54.2	+48 32	16½-inch

Observation: lies 24 sec. of R.A. p. and 2 arc-min S. of NGC 4837. Extremely faint and small. No details noted. Barely visible.
References: MCG, UGC & CGCG - not listed. POSS - plate O-1350, small, slightly extended N.p.-S.f. Shows a definite stellar nucleus but otherwise uniform. S.f. end more narrow than N.p.

A 115	UGC 08085	12 55.8	+14 50	16½-inch

Observation: visible at x84. Very faint, extended N.p.-S.f., narrow and of uniform brightness though central area is a little wider. South are 2 stars which point to it, S. being the brighter.
References: MCG - 3-33-18, Fab, Mp 14.9. UGC - 08085, 2'.5 x 0'.6, SB?c, P.A. 115°, Mp 14.9. CGCG - Anon., Mp 14.9. POSS - plate O-1572, extended system. Bright, elongated central area, no nucleus visible. Ends of extensions quite diffuse, esp. S.f.

A 116	Unlisted	12 59.4	+27 52	16½-inch

Observation: lies 6 sec. of R.A. p. and 1 arc-min S. of NGC 4926. E.f. and can only be distinguished as a small nebulous knot, without any central brightening, f. the southernmost of 2 stars which are p. NGC 4926.
References: MCG, UGC & CGCG - not listed. POSS - plate O-1393, small, elliptical, with major axis aligned S.p.-N.f. No nucleus.

95

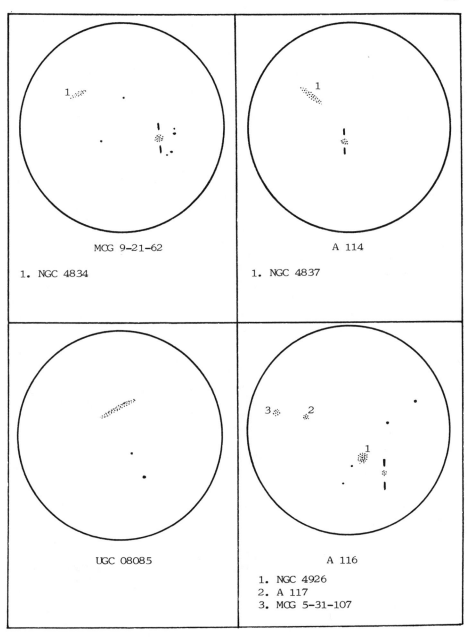

MCG 9-21-62

1. NGC 4834

A 114

1. NGC 4837

UGC 08085

A 116

1. NGC 4926
2. A 117
3. MCG 5-31-107

W.S. No.	Name	R.A.	(1950)	Dec.	Telescope

A 117   MCG 5-31-107   12 59.7   +27 55   16½-inch

Observation: lies 12 sec. of R.A. f. and 2 arc-min N. of NGC 4926.
First noted with x176 as very faint, irreg. round and of uniform
surface brightness. No additional details noted at x351.
References: MCG - 5-31-107, (Ne), Hpb, Mp 15.1. UGC - in Notes
to NGC 4926, 0'.6 x 0'.5, Mp 15.1. CGCG - Anon., Mp 15.1. RNGC -
listed as 4926A. POSS - plate 0-1393, 2nd brightest in group.
Small, sl.el. E-W, with a small envelope. V.f. star off p. edge.

A 118   Unlisted   12 59.7   +27 55   16½-inch

Observation: lies at almost the same co-ordinates as MCG 5-31-107,
actually slightly p. It is extremely faint, barely visible, just
a small knot of nebulosity without any detectable features.
References: MCG, UGC & CGCG - not listed. POSS - plate 0-1393,
compact, slightly extended S.p.-N.f.

A 119   Unlisted   13 01.6   +28 28   16½-inch

Observation: lies 6 sec. of R.A. f. and on the same Dec. as NGC
4944. It is small, extremely faint, just a featureless knot of
uniform surface brightness. It is very close f. and very
slightly N. of the star which is just off f. end of NGC 4944.
References: MCG - not listed. UGC - in Notes to NGC 4944 as a
comp. (0'.4 x 0'.3), P.A. 84°, dist. 1'.1 but this could refer to
a 2nd object also v. close f. CGCG - lists 4944 as a double
system, but no other mention of this object. POSS - plate 0-1393,
shows NGC 4944 with A 119 in position described;at about x6 sep.
of these 2 objects is another, f. A 4th galaxy lies S. NGC 4944.

A 120   MCG 5-31-151   13 09.2   +31 48   16½-inch

Observation: best seen at x176 as faint, very compact, with a
stell. nuc. in small, uniformly bright envelope. Star close S.f.
and another, similarly bright, at a greater distance N.f.
References: MCG - 5-31-151, N; H, Mp 14.0. UGC & CGCG - not
listed. POSS - plate 0-1393, extremely compact, prominent
stellar nucleus.

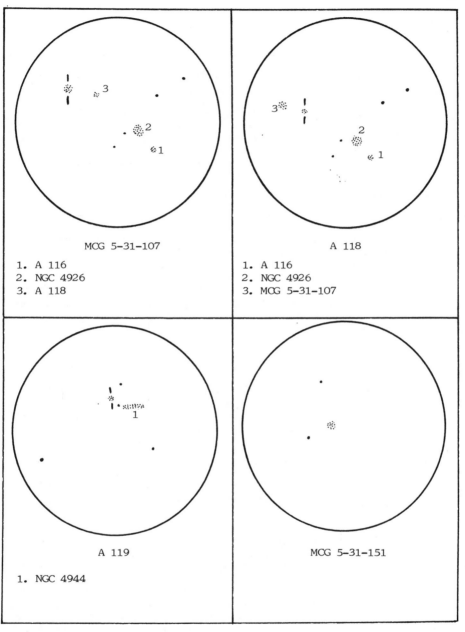

MCG 5-31-107

1. A 116
2. NGC 4926
3. A 118

A 118

1. A 116
2. NGC 4926
3. MCG 5-31-107

A 119

1. NGC 4944

MCG 5-31-151

98

W.S. No.	Name	R.A. (1950) Dec.	Telescope

A 121   UGC 08492   13 27.8   +31 39   16½-inch

Observation: first susp. while examining UGC 08496 at x176. I
continually received a strong impression of a neb. image about ⅓
dist. from UGC 08496 and the 2 stars which lie p. Confirmed at
x351 as very faint, very small and uniformly bright.
References: MCG – 5-32-30, (Ne), Mp 15.0. UGC – 08492, 1'.0 x
0'.9, Compact, Mp 15.0. CGCG – Anon., Mp 15.0. POSS – plate
O-131, small, elliptical, brighter central area.

A 122   UGC 08496   13 28.0   +31 35   16½-inch

Observation: not seen at x84. At x176, it is small, faint,
irregular in shape with no central brightening. Faint star close
p. and a brighter star at a distance N.p.
References: MCG – 5-32-31, Fp; 2sbp; Tab, Mp 14.9. UGC – 08496,
1'.3 x 0'.7, disrupted multiple system, Mp 14.9. CGCG – Anon.,
Mp 14.9. POSS – plate O-131, unusual appearance, irregular with
curved tails p. and f., f. being brighter. Two nuclei in centre,
aligned N-S, S. being brighter.

A 123   UGC 08571   13 33.0   +62 15   16½-inch

Observation: best seen with x176, it is small, very faint and
appears to be extended almost E-W. Uniform surface brightness.
Lies just f. the midpoint between 2 faint stars; there is also a
v.f. star close p. and another S.f.
References: MCG – 10-19-95, F, Mp 14.0. UGC – 08571, 1'.2 x 0'.3,
S, P.A. 67°, Mp 14.1. CGCG – Anon., Mp 14.1. POSS – plate O-704,
extended, major axis S.p.-N.f., narrow towards S.p. end.

A 124   UGC 08621   13 35.5   +39 25   16½-inch

Observation: medium size, fairly bright and irreg. round; at x176
the central lens seen to be brighter than surrounding envelope.
Close N.f. is a coarse double with bright components aligned
S.p.-N.f., f. component slightly the brighter. They point almost
directly towards the galaxy.
References: MCG – 7-28-41, F; Hb, Mp 14.0. UGC – 08621, 0'.8 x
0'.8, S, Mp 14.2. CGCG – Anon., Mp 14.2. POSS – plate O-154,
round with brighter lens in a small envelope.

99

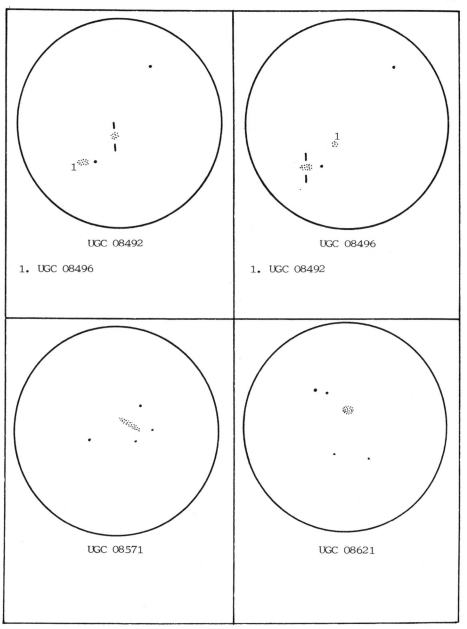

UGC 08492

1. UGC 08496

UGC 08496

1. UGC 08492

UGC 08571

UGC 08621

W.S. No.	Name	R.A. (1950) Dec.	Telescope

A 125   Unlisted   13 59.7   +33 48   16½-inch

Observation: lies 12 sec. of R.A. f. and 16 arc-min S. of NGC
5421. It is the southernmost of the visible group and is very
faint, irregular in shape and slightly brighter in the centre. It
is f. a group of 3 stars.
References: MCG, UGC & CGCG - not listed. RNGC - A 125 is not B
comp. mentioned. POSS - plate O-106, stell. nuc. with small
envelope extended S.p.-N.f.

A 126   UGC 08984   14 01.6   +35 59   16½-inch

Observation: easy at x84. Small, quite bright, needle-shaped
object aligned S.p.-N.f.; only slight evidence of central
brightening. To the N. are 2 stars of similar mag., aligned
almost directly E-W, p. star slightly closer.
References: MCG - 6-31-56, F, Mp 14.0. UGC - 08984, 1'.3 x 0'.3,
S, P.A. 35°, Mp 14.2. CGCG - Anon., Mp 14.2. POSS - plate O-16,
elongated system; slightly brighter centre but no nucleus.

A 127   UGC 09056   14 07.5   +49 16   16½-inch

Observation: visible with x84. Pretty small and quite faint,
narrow, extended N.p.-S.f., brightens in the middle. Centred in
a triangle of stars.
References: MCG - 8-26-05, F; Mp 15.0. UGC - 09056, 1'.1 x 0'.2,
Pec., P.A. 143°, Mp 14.4. CGCG - Anon., Mp 14.4. POSS - plate
O-120, small, uniform, wedge-shaped narrowing at N.p. end.

A 128   UGC 09071   14 08.4   +54 27   16½-inch

Observation: small, extremely faint and very narrow, major axis
aligned S.p.-N.f. Seems to be of uniform surface brightness.
References: MCG - 9-23-46, L?, Dd; H, (288 m), Mp 14.0. UGC -
09071, 2'.2 x 0'.45, Sc, P.A. 37°, Mp 15.1. CGCG - Anon., Mp
15.1. POSS - plate O-1409, elongated central lens with fainter
extensions, no nucleus visible.

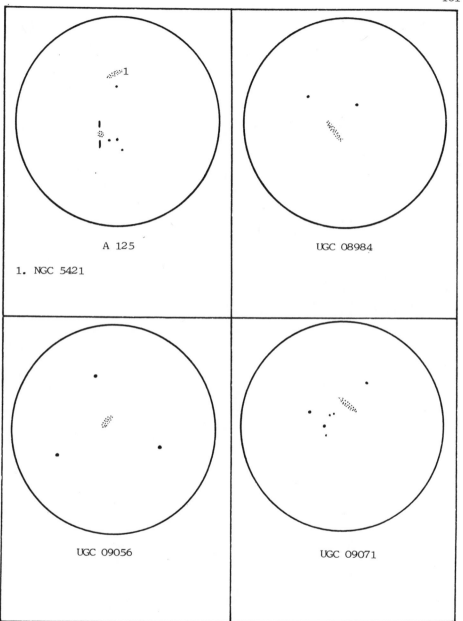

A 125

1. NGC 5421

UGC 08984

UGC 09056

UGC 09071

W.S. No.	Name	R.A. (1950) Dec.		Telescope

A 129   UGC 09266   14 25.2   +30 10   17½-inch*

Observation: only seen with averted vision as a round patch of
nebulosity of even brightness, located somewhat S.p. the field
containing NGC 5642.
References: MCG – 5–34–44, B; Da Ri, H, Mp 15.1. UGC – 09266,
1'.0 x 0'.6, SBc-I, P.A. 165°, Mp 15.4. CGCG – Anon., ZWG
163.053, Mp 15.4. POSS – plate 0–070, small, round, uniform.

A 130   UGC 09302   14 27.0   +32 00   13.1-inch*

Observation: seen only with a.v. as a patch of nebulosity
extended N–S and of even brightness throughout. Star close to p.
edge hinders observation. Very difficult.
References: MCG – 5–34–54, Fc; Mp 15.6. UGC – 09302, 1'.0 x 0'.2,
S-Irr, P.A. 7°, Mp 15.6. CGCG – Anon., ZWG 163.065, Mp 15.6.
POSS – plate 0–070, small, narrow, edge-on, uniform surface
brightness; p. the star SAO 064200.

A 131   MCG 5–34–53   14 27.0   +30 18   17½-inch*

Observation: seen with a.v. at x127 as a round, nebulous knot of
uniform surface brightness. Glimpsed with direct vision.
Similar in size to NGC 5642.
References: MCG – 5–34–53, Ne; Db-Ri, Mp 15.5. UGC – not listed.
CGCG – Anon., ZWG 163.062, Mp 15.5. POSS – plate 0–070, small,
round object of uniform surface brightness close N. of NGC 5642.

A 132   UGC 09425   14 35.6   +30 42   13.1-inch*

Observation: visible at x94, W. of NGC 5709 and in the same field.
It is round and gradually brightens in the middle. Easier than
NGC 5709 and appears to be about twice as large.
References: MCG – 5–34–83, N;C-Ne; 28₂oz, Mp 15.0. UGC – 09425,
1'.0 x 0'.4, Double system, connected, plumes, Mp 15.0. CGCG –
Anon., double system, tidal effect, ZWG 163.089, Mp 15.0. POSS –
plate 0–070, sl.el. N.p.–S.f., outer env. suggests some spiral
structure, brighter bar nucleus.

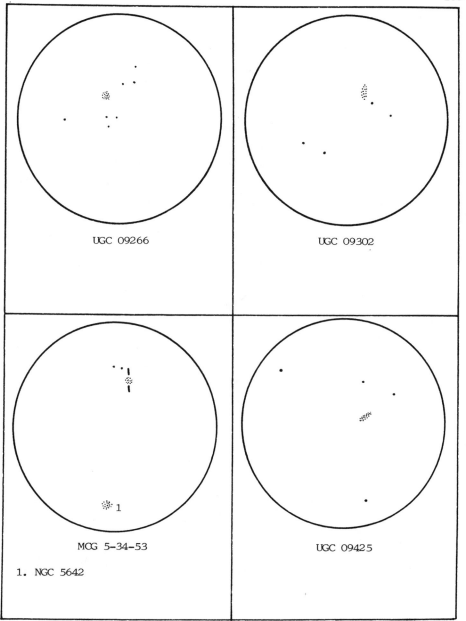

UGC 09266

UGC 09302

MCG 5-34-53

※ 1

UGC 09425

1. NGC 5642

W.S. No.	Name	R.A. (1950) Dec.	Telescope

A 133   MCG 4-37-21   15 38.0   +21 41   16½-inch

Observation: lies 12 sec. of R.A. f. and 3 arc-min N. of NGC
5975. First noticed at x176 as a small, faint nebulous knot to
the N. of a pretty bright star.
References: MCG - 4-37-21, Ne; 2B Rab, (2₿₴-R), Mp 14.5. UGC -
mentioned in Notes: 0'.8 x 0'.8, Mp 15.2. CGCG - Anon., Mp 15.2.
POSS - plate O-1119, small, stell. nuc. in rectangular envelope
with e.f. star on N.f. edge. Faint spiral structure visible on
p. and f. sides, almost a ring.

A 134   MCG 7-34-48   16 25.9   +40 47   16½-inch

Observation: lies 6 sec. of R.A. p. and 15 arc-min S. of NGC
6160. First suspected at x351; it is e.f. and irregular in shape.
Faint star S.f., ¾ distance between the two galaxies.
References: MCG - 7-34-48, (N)?, H, Mp 15.1. UGC - in Notes, P.A.
185°. CGCG - Anon., Mp 15.7. POSS - plate O-743, very small and
faint, stell. nuc. with small envelope.

A 135   MCG 6-36-45   16 26.5   +33 19   16½-inch

Observation: lies on same R.A. and 21 arc-min N. of NGC 6162.
Extremely faint, irreg. round and of uniform brightness. There
is a dbl. star N. (aligned E-W) and group of 4 stars f.
References: MCG - 6-36-45, L, 1Scb, 1Sc, Mp 15.0. UGC - not
listed. CGCG - Anon., Mp 15.6. POSS - plate O-1093, almost
triangular, like a flat-iron, stell. nuc., brighter area at S.p.

A 136   MCG 7-34-55   16 26.9   +39 37   16½-inch

Observation: lies on same R.A. and 1 arc-min S. of NGC 6166. It
is v. small, v. faint but a definite nebular image. Lies between
NGC 6166 and MCG 7-34-64, but slightly closer to NGC 6166.
References: MCG - 7-34-55, Ne, Mp 16.0. UGC & CGCG - not listed.
RNGC - it is not one of the anon. objects listed as companions of
NGC 6166. POSS - plate O-743, stellar, compact. Brighter centre
with a very small envelope.

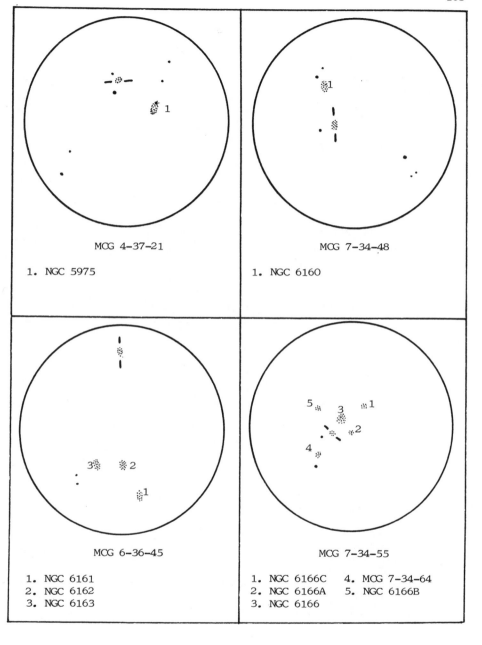

MCG 4-37-21

1. NGC 5975

MCG 7-34-48

1. NGC 6160

MCG 6-36-45

1. NGC 6161
2. NGC 6162
3. NGC 6163

MCG 7-34-55

1. NGC 6166C   4. MCG 7-34-64
2. NGC 6166A   5. NGC 6166B
3. NGC 6166

W.S. No.	Name	R.A. (1950) Dec.	Telescope

A 137   MCG 7-34-64   16 27.0   +39 36   16½-inch

Observation: lies 6 sec. of R.A. f. and 4 arc-min S. of NGC 6166.
It is v.f., irregularly round and of uniform surface brightness.
Close S.f. is a star about ½ distance separating it from NGC 6166.
References: MCG - 7-34-64, Nn, Dab, Mp 15.0. UGC - not listed.
CGCG - Anon., Mp 15.4. RNGC - not listed. POSS - plate O-743,
small, stellar nucleus within a small envelope.

A 138   UGC 10427   16 28.7   +41 13   16½-inch

Observation: p. of 3 anon. galaxies in the field. It is very
faint, irreg. in shape and of uniform surface brightness. Curved
line of 3 stars S.p., S. brightest and N. closest. A brightish
star lies p. this N. star.
References: MCG - 7-34-91, Fa; D, (999), Mp 15.0. UGC - 10427,
1'.5 x 1'.3, SBc, Mp 15.4. CGCG - Anon., diffuse spiral, Mp 15.4
POSS - plate O-743, small, br. centre, v.f. outer ring structure.

A 139   UGC 10432   16 29.0   +41 19   16½-inch

Observation: while observing UGC 10427 at x351, I strongly
suspected a nebular image S.f. It is a barely visible small knot
of nebulosity of uniform surface brightness.
References: MCG - 7-34-98, L; A; 21a, Mp 16.0. UGC - 10432, Sb,
1'.5 x 0'.2, Mp 16.0. CGCG - not listed. POSS - plate O-743,
v. sm. spindle, major axis aligned almost N-S, stell. nuc., S.
extension is wider at the end than the N. extension.

A 140   UGC 10436   16 29.4   +41 16   16½-inch

Observation: f. of 3; it is faint but visible at x84 and seen to
be of medium size and irregularly round. S.f. are 2 stars
aligned almost directly N-S. Better seen with x176.
References: MCG - 7-34-103, B?, D;Rb; 18 c;228b; H; Mp 14.0.
UGC - 10436, 1'.4 x 1'.4, Sc, Mp 14.8. CGCG - Anon., Mp 14.8.
POSS - plate O-743, face-on spiral with developed lens and
diffuse outer envelope. Prominent curved arm emerges from N.p.
edge, curving to N.

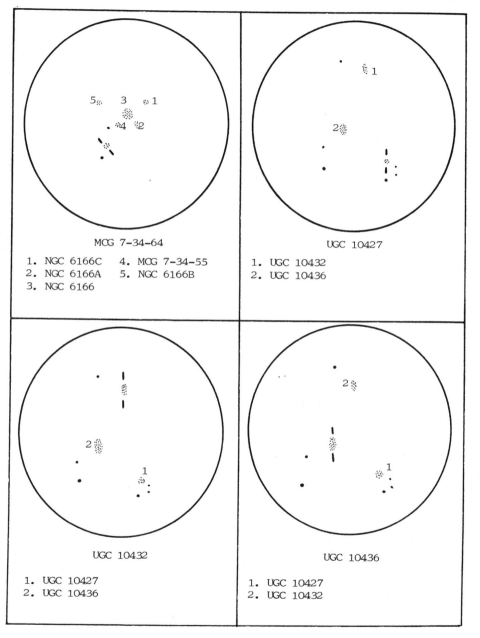

MCG 7-34-64

1. NGC 6166C 4. MCG 7-34-55
2. NGC 6166A 5. NGC 6166B
3. NGC 6166

UGC 10427

1. UGC 10432
2. UGC 10436

UGC 10432

1. UGC 10427
2. UGC 10436

UGC 10436

1. UGC 10427
2. UGC 10432

W.S. No.	Name	R.A. (1950) Dec.		Telescope

| A 141 | MCG 7-34-130 | 16 38.8 | +39 25 | 16½-inch |

Observation: first of 2 visible in field at x84; it is v. small, faint, irreg. round with a small stellar nucleus. Lies between 2 stars aligned almost N-S, but closer to brighter, S. star. References: MCG - 7-34-130, N; H, Mp 14.0. UGC - not listed. CGCG - Anon., Mp 15.1. POSS - plate O-743, small, brighter env., with very short, faint, outer nebulous 'wings'.

| A 142 | MCG 7-34-131 | 16 38.8 | +39 20 | 16½-inch |

Observation: lies S. of A 141 and is very faint, irregular in shape, perhaps sl. el. S.p.-N.f., and of uniform surface brightness. More elongated than A 141. V.f. star close to N.f. end. References: MCG - 7-34-131, Fc, Mp 15.0. UGC - not listed. CGCG - Anon., Mp 15.6. POSS - plate O-743, small, elongated system, brighter centre; other fainter galaxies in vicinity.

| A 143 | UGC 10523 | 16 41.6 | +42 16 | 16½-inch |

Observation: extremely faint, requiring x176 to identify, small, elongated almost N-S and of uniform surface brightness. Bright star at a distance N.; 2 stars aligned S.p.-N.f. closer S.f. References: MCG - 7-34-141, L; $\Theta\Theta$ bc, Mp 15.0. UGC - 10523, S, 1'.3 x 0'.35, P.A. 174°, Mp 15.3. CGCG - Anon., Mp 15.3. POSS - plate O-743, small, el. as described, stell. nuc. with 'wings' either side. Very faint star close S.f.

| A 144 | UGC 10544 | 16 44.9 | +36 10 | 16½-inch |

Observation: barely visible at x84 and really required x351 for positive identification. Extremely faint, very small and el. N-S. No central brightening detected. V.f. star S.f. References: MCG 6-37-8, L; Da; R-af, Mp 14.0. UGC - 10544, Sa, 1'.0 x 0'.45, P.A. 177°, Mp 15.4. CGCG - Anon., Mp 15.4. POSS - plate O-1069, small, elongated N-S. Bright, small, extended lens with 'wings'.

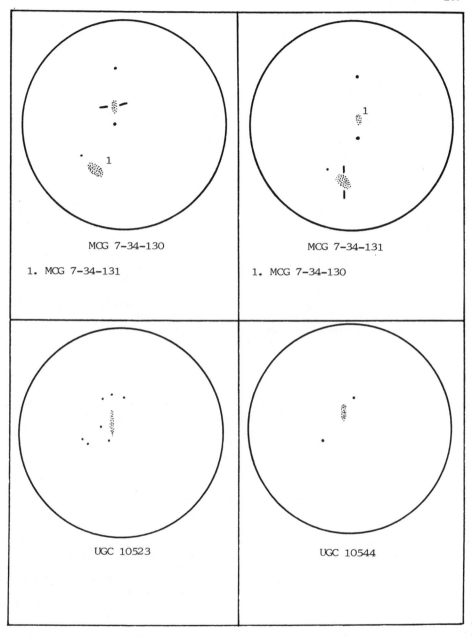

MCG 7-34-130

1. MCG 7-34-131

MCG 7-34-131

1. MCG 7-34-130

UGC 10523

UGC 10544

W.S. No.	Name	R.A. (1950) Dec.	Telescope
A 145	UGC 10545	16 45.0 +34 30	16½-inch

Observation: extremely faint, small, appears to be elongated N-S and uniform in brightness. No bright stars close by, the nearest being N. and slightly f. Very difficult.
References: MCG – 6-37-9, Lp, 1℮ fco, 1℮ bo, Mp 15.1. UGC – 10545, 1'.0 x 0'.4, Sb-c, P.A. 156°, Mp 15.1. CGCG – Anon., Mp 15.1. POSS – plate O-1069, extended slightly N.p.-S.f. Has well developed lens with spiral extensions. S.f. extension clearest.

| A 146 | UGC 10547 | 16 45.1   +34 15 | 16½-inch |

Observation: faint but vis. at x84. Irreg. round with slightly brighter centre; resembles a small planetary nebula with its br. centre and ill-defined outer edges. Lies f. southernmost of 2 stars aligned S.p.-N.f.
References: MCG – 6-37-10, L; Is, 1Sb, H, Mp 14.0. UGC – 10547, 1'.5 x 0'.7, SBb, Mp 14.7. CGCG – Anon., Mp 14.7. POSS – plate O-1069, extended system with inner brighter bar aligned N.N.p. – S.S.f. contained within an outer envelope aligned N-S.

| A 147 | UGC 10553 | 16 45.6   +40 20 | 16½-inch |

Observation: requires x176 to identify; it is small, quite narrow, elongated N.p.-S.f. Brightens in the middle but not to a nucleus. S.f. are 3 stars in a line; central has a companion N.p. and these point towards the galaxy.
References: MCG – 7-34-149, F;2℮a, Mp 14.0. UGC – 10553, 1'.1 x 0'.5, SBa-b, P.A. 153°, Mp 15.0. CGCG – Anon., Mp 15.0. POSS – plate O-743, extended with small br. nuc., N.p. extension most br.

| A 148 | UGC 10571 | 16 47.8   +48 43 | 16½-inch |

Observation: e.f. but visible at x84; it is small, quite narrow, extended S.p.-N.f., with no central brightening. There are 3 faint stars close p., aligned S.p.-N.f.
References: MCG – 8-31-2, L?, 2℮b, Mp 15.0. UGC – 10571, SBc, 1'.3 x 0'.35, P.A. 12°, Mp 15.4. CGCG – Anon., Mp 15.4. POSS – plate O-1370, elongated system with an extended lens, aligned N-S, surrounded by a diffuse envelope S.p.-N.f.

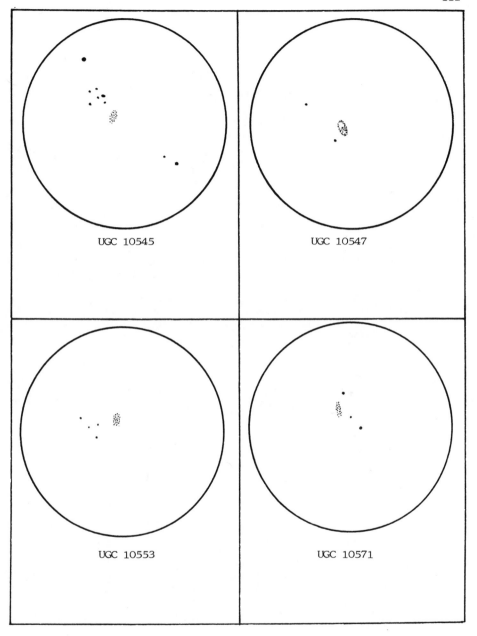

UGC 10545

UGC 10547

UGC 10553

UGC 10571

W.S. No.	Name	R.A. (1950) Dec.		Telescope

A 149   UGC 10584   16 49.2   +55 28   16½-inch

Observation: easily visible with x84. Quite bright, irregular
in shape with a stell. nuc. Bright star just off N.p. edge makes
object appear like a nebulous flare attached to the star. Nebula
aligned S.p.-N.f. NGC 6246 in same field N. and slightly p.
References: MCG - 9-27-101, n, 2Scb, Da; SSb, SSd, Mp 13.0. UGC
10584, 2'.5 x 2'.5, Sc/SBc, Mp 14.7. CGCG - Anon., Mp 14.7.
POSS - plate O-1101, quite large spiral almost face-on showing a
large amount of detail and with a number of stars superimposed.

A 150   UGC 10589   16 49.4   +55 55   16½-inch

Observation: v.f. but visible with x84; it is of medium size,
uniform surface brightness and el. almost E-W. Seems wider at p.
end while f. end tapers to a point. Lies between 2 faint stars,
being a little closer to the p. star.
References: MCG - 9-27-102, Pc:, Mp 14.0. UGC - 10589, 1'.8 x
0'.7, Pec., P.A. 62°, Mp 15.4. CGCG - Anon., Mp 15.4. POSS -
plate O-1101, el., br. central lens with diffuse extensions.

A 151   UGC 10593   16 51.3   +55 59   16½-inch

Observation: e.f. but visible at x84; it is small, quite narrow,
elongated almost E-W, and shows only slight central brightening.
Pretty br. star at a distance S.f., v.f. star close p. which is
one of a triangle of stars enclosing the galaxy.
References: MCG - 9-28-1, N; Da, Mp 15.0. UGC - 10593, 1'.5 x
0'.5, Sa-b, P.A. 87°, Mp 15.2. CGCG - plate O-765, el. E-W,
diffuse outer envelope enclosing and extended lens.

A 152   CGCG Anon.   17 14.5   +57 30   16½-inch

Observation: lies on same R.A. and 1 arc-min N. of NGC 6338.
Only seen at x351 as an e.f. compact knot, uniformly bright.
References: MCG - confuses position for NGC 6345 for position of
this anon. MCG 10-24-117 should be for anon., not NGC 6338.
UGC - in Notes for UGC 10784. CGCG - Anon., dbl. nuc., Mp 15.6.
RNGC - in Notes (8). POSS - plate O-1414, most N. of 4 aligned
N-S. Small, diffuse env. surrounding double nucleus.

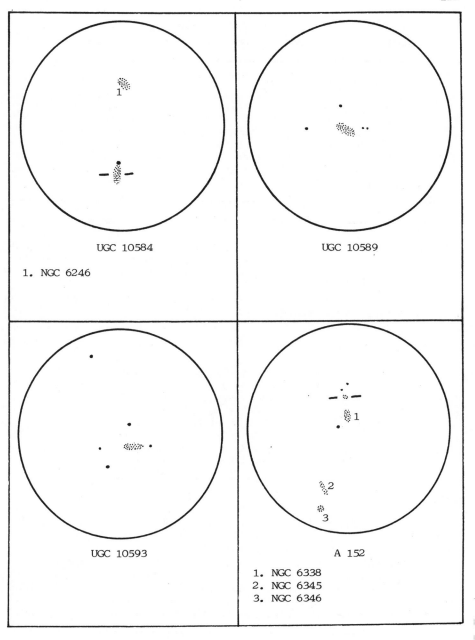

UGC 10584

1. NGC 6246

UGC 10589

UGC 10593

A 152

1. NGC 6338
2. NGC 6345
3. NGC 6346

W.S. No.	Name	R.A. (1950) Dec.	Telescope

A 153   UGC 11635   20 46.0   +79 58   16½-inch

Observation: very faint, medium size, irregular in shape and
slightly elongated S.p.-N.f. Perhaps a little brighter in the
centre. Lies within a triangle of faint stars.
References: MCG - 13-15-1, L; SSbf, Mp 13.0. UGC - 11635, Sb,
3'.5 x 1'.3, P.A. 35°, Mp 14.2. CGCG - Anon., Mp 14.2. POSS -
plate 0-1232, quite large, extended spiral. Small nucleus, large
lens and diffuse spiral arms.

A 154   UGC 11760   21 29.2   +02 15   16½-inch

Observation: lies 18 sec. of R.A. f. and 1 arc-min S. of NGC 7081.
E.f., just a patch of diffuse nebulosity first seen at x176. Two
stars close N., aligned N.p.-S.f., point towards NGC 7081.
References: MCG - 0-55-2, N;1s, Hc, Mp 14.2. UGC - 11760, 1'.1 x
0'.9, S, Mp 14.6. CGCG - Anon., Mp 14.6. RNGC - in Notes (8) on
Pec. companion 2' S.f.

A 155   Unlisted   22 07.9   +40 46   16½-inch

Observation: lies 3 sec. of R.A. p. and 40 arc-sec N. of NGC
7223. First seen at x351 as a v. sm., v.f. knot of nebulosity
very close N.p. NGC 7223. Very close to N. of 3 stars.
References: MCG, UGC & CGCG - not listed. POSS - plate 0-580,
as described, just p. N. star of 3, it should not be confused
with the other objects listed in UGC which lie S.p. & N.f. 7223.
V. sm., el. N-S, with stell. nuc. Could be H II region but if so
is brighter than nuc. and the rest of the nearest spiral arm.

A 156   UGC 11973   22 14.7   +41 15   16½-inch

Observation: faint but easily seen at x84, though better at x176
when it is found to be of medium size, elongated S.p.-N.f. and
brightens slightly in the middle to an extended core. Lies
between 2 stars aligned S.p.-N.f., former has faint comp. N.
References: MCG - 7-45-23, BBb, 2Sc, Mp 14.0. UGC - 11973, 3'.3
x 0'.9, Sb/SBc, P.A. 42°, Mp 13.5. CGCG - Anon., Mp 13.5. POSS
plate 0-580, large bright central area with an inner bright
spiral arm, esp. on N.f. edge; fainter arms visible beyond this.

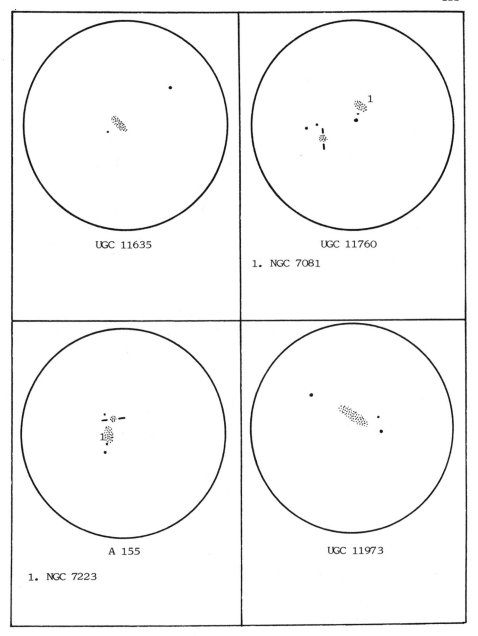

UGC 11635

UGC 11760

1. NGC 7081

A 155

1. NGC 7223

UGC 11973

W.S. No.	Name	R.A. (1950) Dec.	Telescope
A 157	UGC 11994	22 18.6 +33 03	16½-inch

Observation: extremely faint; first seen at x176 as a small, narrow nebulous streak, el. N.p.-S.f., of uniform surface brightness. Lies between 2 faint stars aligned S.p.-N.f. References: MCG - 5-52-012, Fbc, A, Mp 14.0. UGC - 11994, 2'.5 x 0'.3, Sb-c, P.A. 122°, Mp 15.0. CGCG - Anon., Mp 15.0. POSS - plate O-383, lies in rich field of faint stars. Edge-on, narrow, central lens extended in direction of major axis.

| A 158 | UGC 11995 | 22 18.9   +36 20 | 16½-inch |

Observation: very faint and, although just visible with x84, is better seen at x176. It is small, narrow, el. N.p.-S.f. and brightens in the middle but not to a nucleus. Bright star 16 arc-min f.; close f. is a curved line of 3 v.f. stars. References: MCG - not listed. UGC - 11995, 1'.6 x 0'.2, Sa, P.A. 141°, Mp 14.8. CGCG - Anon., Mp 14.8. POSS - plate O-778, small developed core with very narrow extensions N.p.-S.f.

| A 159 | UGC 12007 | 22 20.3   +35 57 | 16½-inch |

Observation: lies 18 sec. of R.A. f. and 1 arc-min S. of NGC 7265. It is v.f., quite small, extended S.p.-N.f. and of uniform surface brightness. Requires x351 to detect. Star involved which is most f. of a Sagitta-like group of stars S.f. NGC 7265. References: MCG - 6-49-9, L?, H+*?, Mp 14.0. UGC - 12007, 1'.4 x 1'.1, Mp 15.3 (Notes describes it as pear-shaped). CGCG - Anon., star superimposed, Mp 15.3. POSS - plate O-778, confirms above observation; it has incomplete diff. arms at ends of major axis.

| A 160 | CGCG Anon. | 22 20.8   +36 08 | 16½-inch |

Observation: lies 38 sec. of R.A. f. and 10 arc-min S. of NGC 7265. Easily visible, quite bright, irregular, brightens slightly in the middle. Possibly sl. el. N.p.-S.f. Lies S.f. a triangle of faint stars, p. the apex star. References: MCG & UGC - not listed. CGCG - Anon., Mp 15.3. POSS plate O-778, el. N.p.-S.f. as described. The p. end is wider than f. and the nucleus appears to be a little eccentric towards the p. end.

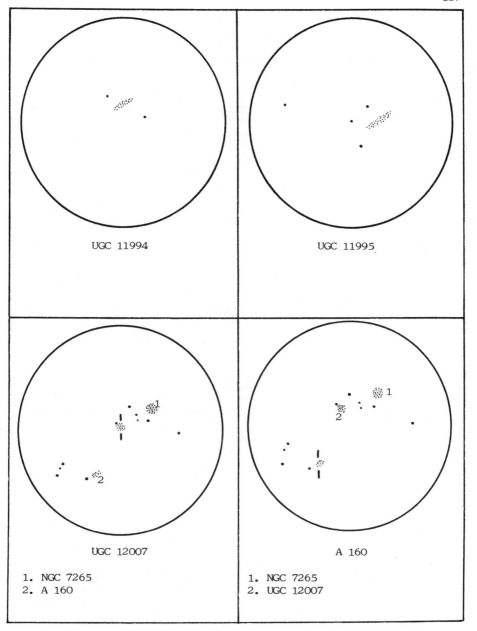

UGC 11994

UGC 11995

UGC 12007

1. NGC 7265
2. A 160

A 160

1. NGC 7265
2. UGC 12007

W.S. No.	Name	R.A. (1950) Dec.	Telescope

A 161   UGC 12012   22 20.8   +35 35   13.1-inch*

Observation: at x127, located at opposite edge of field to NGC
7265. Best seen at x147 when found to be small, faint, of uniform
surface brightness and extended N.f.-S.p.
References: MCG - 6-49-10, L→Db, Mp 15.0. UGC - 12012, 1'.0 x
0'.6, Sb, P.A. 133°, Mp 15.3. CGCG - Anon., ZWG 514.020, Mp 15.3.
POSS - plate 0-778, small,oval outer envelope, extended N.p.-S.f.
Brighter middle region.

A 162   MCG 6-49-56   22 36.1   +35 08   16½-inch

Observation: lies 12 sec. of R.A. f. and 7 arc-min S. of NGC 7342.
Best seen at x176 as small and narrow; central region brightens
but not to a nucleus. Bright star N.f. and a faint one midway
between MCG 6-49-56 and nearby UGC 12127 (MCG 6-49-58).
References: MCG - 6-49-56, Fa, Mp 15.0. UGC - in Notes as 0'.8 x
0'.2, SO-A, Mp 15.4. CGCG - Anon., Mp 15.4. POSS - plate 0-778,
sl. el. S.p.-N.f., stell. nuc. with short extensions.

A 163   UGC 12127   22 36.2   +35 05   16½-inch

Observation: lies 18 sec. of R.A. f. and 10 arc-min S of NGC 7342.
Brighter than MCG 6-49-56 and easily seen with x84. It is irreg.
round, quite bright and brightens to a small core in the centre.
References: MCG - 6-49-58, Elliptical, Mp 14.0. UGC - 12127,
1'.5 x 1'.5, Elliptical (brightest in group), Mp 15.0. CGCG -
Anon., Mp 15.0. POSS - plate 0-778, elliptical with env., small
knot or star invested in S.f. end.

A 164   MCG 6-49-60   22 36.3   +35 06   16½-inch

Observation: 3rd of 4; lies 24 sec. of R.A. f. and 9 arc-min S.
of NGC 7342. It is faint, irreg. round and uniformly bright
except for very slight central brightening. S. of the faint star
f. that between MCG 6-49-56 and UGC 12127.
References: MCG - 6-49-60, N;H, Mp 16.0. UGC & CGCG - not listed.
POSS - plate 0-778, compact, very small envelope visible.

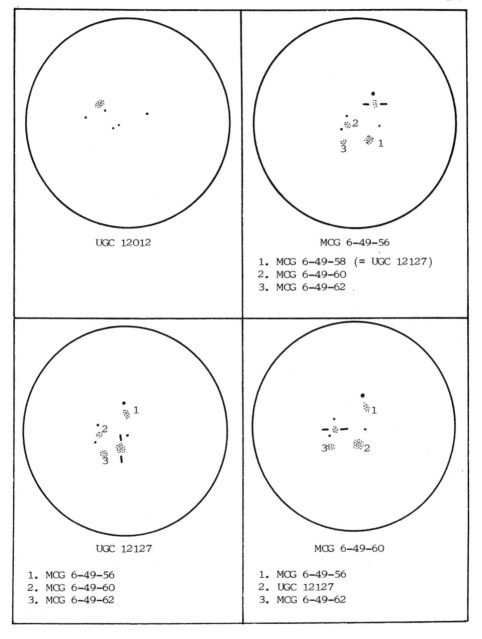

UGC 12012

MCG 6-49-56

1. MCG 6-49-58 (= UGC 12127)
2. MCG 6-49-60
3. MCG 6-49-62 .

UGC 12127

1. MCG 6-49-56
2. MCG 6-49-60
3. MCG 6-49-62

MCG 6-49-60

1. MCG 6-49-56
2. UGC 12127
3. MCG 6-49-62

W.S. No.	Name	R.A. (1950) Dec.	Telescope
A 165	MCG 6-49-62	22 36.4 +35 05	16½-inch

Observation: 4th of 4; it lies 30 sec. of R.A. f. and 10 arc-min S. of NGC 7342, and is directly f. UGC 12127. It is very small and very faint, just a nebulous knot. Diffuse, without any visible central brightening.
References: MCG - 6-49-62, N;H, Mp 16.0. UGC & CGCG - not listed. POSS - plate O-778, very compact, smaller than 6-49-60. Round with a very small envelope. Stellar lens or nucleus.

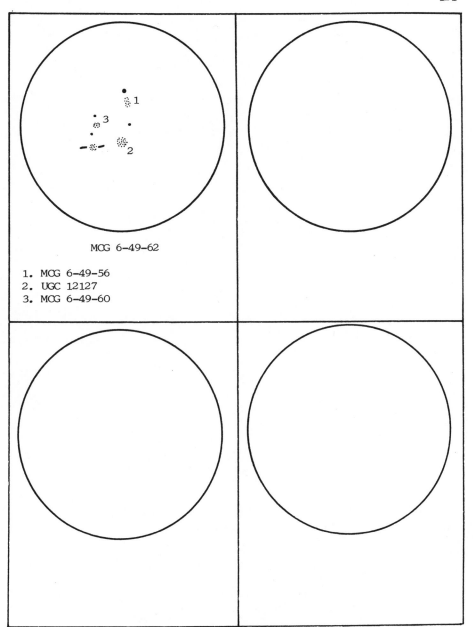

MCG 6-49-62

1. MCG 6-49-56
2. UGC 12127
3. MCG 6-49-60

Catalogue

SECTION 2: TELESCOPE FIELD DRAWINGS.

The following 29 field drawings were made at the telescope by
Ronald J. Morales from his Sonora Desert Observatory. The objects
are also described in detail in Section 1 of the Catalogue, where they
are presented with field charts extracted from the Palomar Observatory
Sky Survey.

The anonymous galaxies in Section 2 can be found on the following
pages in the main Catalogue:

Identification	A No.	Cat. Page No.
UGC 01866	006	40 & 41
UGC 02927	010	42 & 43
UGC 02931	011	42 & 43
UGC 02949	012	42 & 43
MCG 0-12-051	015	44 & 45
MCG 0-12-054	016	44 & 45
MCG -2-14-004	018	46 & 47
UGC 03803	019	46 & 47
UGC 03827	020	46 & 47
UGC 03995	023	48 & 49
MCG 5-19-10	026	50 & 51
UGC 04038	028	50 & 51
MCG 3-27-12	075	74 & 75
UGC 05622	076	74 & 75
UGC 05903	085	80 & 81
UGC 05958	086	80 & 81
UGC 06276	088	80 & 81
UGC 06355	089	82 & 83
UGC 06367	090	82 & 83
UGC 06658	098	86 & 87
UGC 06670	100	86 & 87
UGC 06697	102	88 & 89
UGC 06753	104	88 & 89
MCG 6-26-43	106	90 & 91
UGC 09266	129	102 & 103
UGC 09302	130	102 & 103
MCG 5-34-53	131	102 & 103
UGC 09425	132	102 & 103
UGC 12012	161	118 & 119

N.B. All field drawings are inverted, i.e., N. at the bottom, f. to the
right.

124

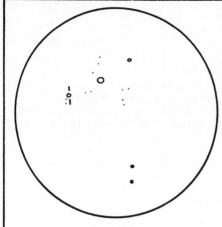

UGC 01866

Telescope: 13.1-inch, f/4.5
Ocular: 10.2mm (= x147). Field 17'
Other Names: MCG +07-6-011
ZWG 539.012

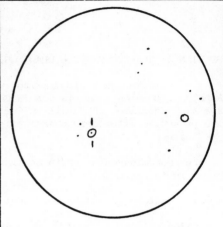

UGC 02927

Telescope: 13.1-inch, f/4.5
Ocular: 8mm (= x187). Field 13'
Other Names: MCG +04-10-006
ZWG 487.007

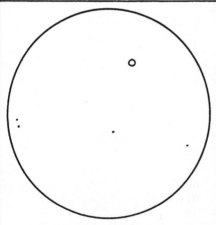

UGC 02931

Telescope: 13.1-inch, f/4.5
Ocular: 10.2mm (= x147). Field 17'
Other Names: MCG +04-10-010
ZWG 487.011

UGC 02949

Telescope: 13.1-inch, f/4.5
Ocular: 10.2mm (= x147). Field 17'
Other Names: MCG +04-10-019
ZWG 487.019

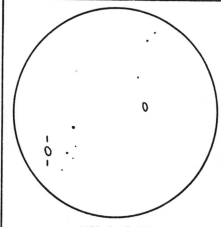

MCG 0-12-051

Telescope: 13.1-inch, f/4.5
Ocular: 10.2mm (=x147). Field 17'
Other Names: ZWG 393.044

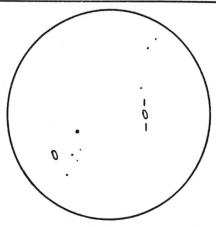

MCG 0-12-054

Telescope: 13.1-inch, f/4.5
Ocular: 10.2mm (=x147). Field 17'
Other Names: ZWG 393.045

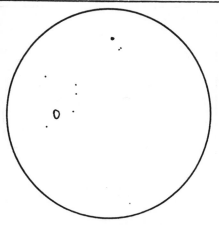

MCG -2-14-004

Telescope: 10-inch, f/5.6
Ocular: 16mm (= x89). Field 21'
Other Names: A 0509-14 (Second Ref.
Catalogue of Bright Galaxies, 1976,
p. 104)

UGC 03803

Telescope: 13.1-inch, f/4.5
Ocular: 8mm (= x187). Field 13'
Other Names: MCG +4-18-002
            ZWG 117.009

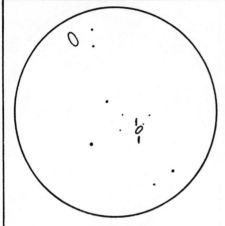

UGC 03827

Telescope: 13.1-inch, f/4.5
Ocular: 10.2mm (=x147). Field 17'
Other Names: MCG +4-18-013
             ZWG 117.029

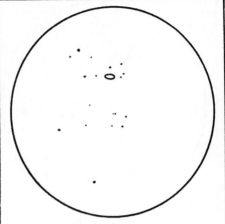

UGC 03995

Telescope: 13.1-inch, f/4.5
Ocular: 8mm (= x187). Field 13'
Other Names: MCG +5-19-001
             ZWG 148.037

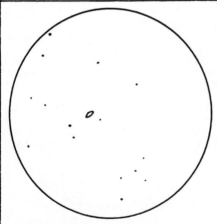

MCG 5-19-10

Telescope: 13.1-inch, f/4.5
Ocular: 8mm (= x187). Field 13'
Other Names: ZWG 148.031

UGC 04038

Telescope: 13.1-inch, f/4.5
Ocular: 8mm (= x187). Field 13'
Other Names: MCG +5-19-013
             ZWG 148.037

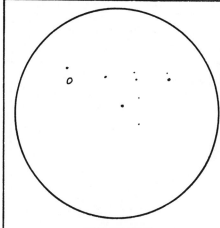

MCG 3-27-12

Telescope: 17.5-inch, f/4.5
Ocular: 16mm (= x125). Field 21'
Other Names: ZWG 94.020

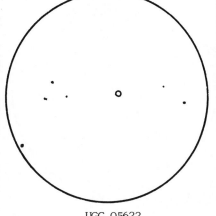

UGC 05622

Telescope: 13.1-inch, f/4.5
Ocular: 10.2mm (=x147). Field 17'
Other Names: MCG 6-23-11
ZWG 183.020

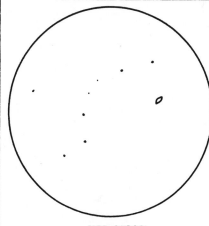

UGC 05903

Telescope: 13.1-inch, f/4.5
Ocular: 10.2mm (=x147). Field 17'
Other Names: MCG +5-26-11
ZWG 155.014

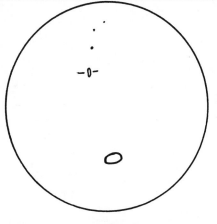

UGC 05958

Telescope: 13.1-inch, f/4.5
Ocular: 10.2mm (=x147). Field 17'
Other Names: MCG +5-26-22
ZWG 155.028

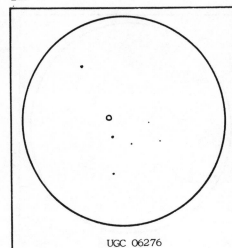

UGC 06276

Telescope: 17.5-inch, f/4.5
Ocular: 12mm (= x167). Field 17'
Other Names: MCG 5-27-32
               ZWG 156.036

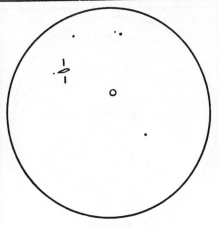

UGC 06355

Telescope: 17.5-inch, f/4.5
Ocular: 12mm (= x167). Field 17'
Other Names: MCG 5-27-059
               ZWG 156.065

UGC 06367

Telescope: 17.5-inch, f/4.5
Ocular: 12mm (= x167). Field 17'
Other Names: MCG 5-27-060
               ZWG 156.066

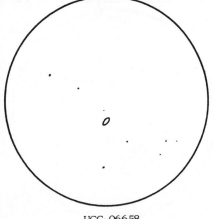

UGC 06658

Telescope: 13.1-inch, f/4.5
Ocular: 10.2mm (=x147). Field 17'
Other Names: MCG 5-28-16
               ZWG 157.016

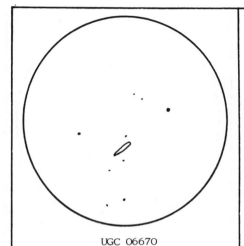

UGC 06670

Telescope: 13.1-inch, f/4.5.
Ocular: 10.2mm (=x147). Field 17'
Other Names: MCG 3-30-53
            ZWG 97.067

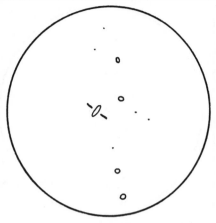

UGC 06697

Telescope: 13.1-inch, f/4.5
Ocular: 10.2mm (=x147). Field 17'
Other Names: MCG 3-30-066
            ZWG 97.087

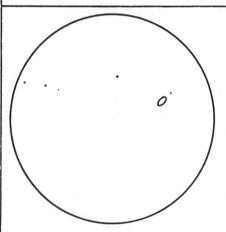

UGC 06753

Telescope: 17.5-inch, f/4.5
Ocular: 10.2mm (=x196). Field 13'
Other Names: MCG 3-30-110
            ZWG 97.146

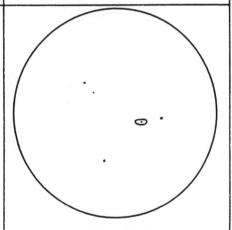

MCG 6-26-43

Telescope: 17.5-inch, f/4.5
Ocular: 16mm (= x125). Field 21'
Other Names: ZWG 186.056

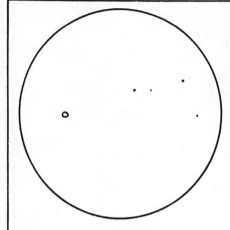

UGC 09266

Telescope: 17.5-inch, f/4.5
Ocular: 12mm (= x167). Field 17'
Other Names: MCG 5-34-44
            ZWG 163.053

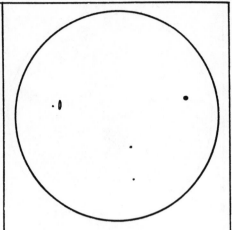

UGC 09302

Telescope: 17.5-inch, f/4.5
Ocular: 12mm (= x167). Field 17'
Other Names: MCG 5-34-54
            ZWG 163.065

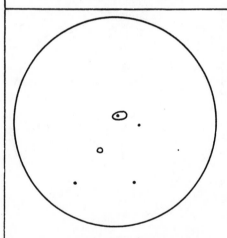

MCG 5-34-53

Telescope: 17.5-inch, f/4.5
Ocular: 12mm (= x167). Field 17'
Other Names: ZWG 163.062

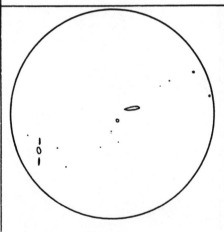

UGC 09425

Telescope: 17.5-inch, f/4.5
Ocular: 16mm (= x125). Field 21'
Other Names: MCG 5-34-83
            ZWG 163.089

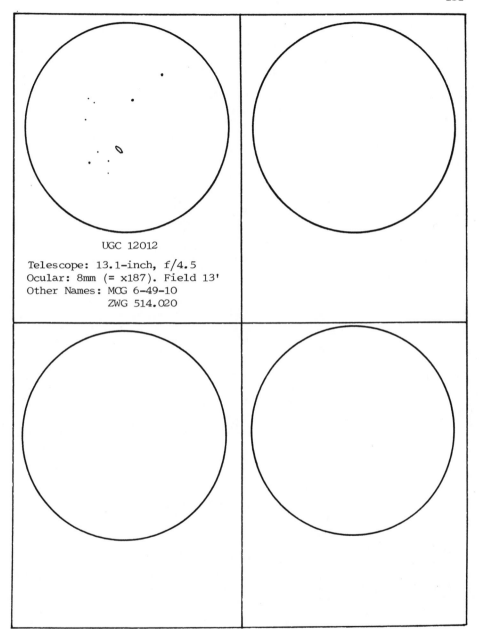

UGC 12012

Telescope: 13.1-inch, f/4.5
Ocular: 8mm (= x187). Field 13'
Other Names: MCG 6-49-10
ZWG 514.020

Catalogue

SECTION 3: ANONYMOUS GALAXY CO—ORDINATES FOR EPOCH 2000.0

W.S. No.	R.A.		Dec.		W.S. No.	R.A.		Dec.	
A 001	00h	07.9m	+33°	00'	A 036	08h	33.1m	+41°	06'
A 002	00	48.8	+31	59	A 037	08	33.3	+41	16
A 003	01	21.1	+40	28	A 038	08	33.5	+41	32
A 004	01	24.8	+33	20	A 039	08	37.3	+40	03
A 005	01	33.3	+62	23	A 040	08	45.6	+36	57
A 006	02	25.2	+41	52	A 041	08	52.1	+52	53
A 007	02	34.8	+32	52	A 042	08	51.9	+16	57
A 008	02	38.7	+40	43	A 043	08	54.9	+49	08
A 009	03	30.0	−05	32	A 044	08	55.0	+49	09
A 010	04	01.6	+23	07	A 045	09	00.3	+52	31
A 011	04	02.3	+25	49	A 046	09	00.5	+51	14
A 012	04	05.0	+25	16	A 047	09	00.2	+35	43
A 013	04	34.1	+73	18	A 048	09	00.6	+50	42
A 014	04	34.3	+73	13	A 049	09	01.9	+60	10
A 015	04	36.3	+03	04	A 050	09	07.7	+66	35
A 016	04	36.4	−02	53	A 051	09	14.7	+40	54
A 017	04	43.1	+00	44	A 052	09	18.1	+79	07
A 018	05	11.5	−14	49	A 053	09	17.2	+41	55
A 019	07	19.9	+22	06	A 054	09	20.8	+33	44
A 020	07	23.2	+22	13	A 055	09	23.4	−10	25
A 021	07	37.6	+35	37	A 056	09	29.6	+62	33
A 022	07	38.5	+37	39	A 057	06	46.5	+45	47
A 023	07	44.1	+29	14	A 058	10	01.2	+55	43
A 024	07	49.4	+74	20	A 059	10	02.5	+53	52
A 025	07	50.9	+74	21	A 060	10	02.5	+32	42
A 026	07	48.9	+28	54	A 061	10	05.9	+58	49
A 027	07	51.7	+72	02	A 062	10	07.3	+47	02
A 028	07	49.6	+26	55	A 063	10	08.2	+53	05
A 029	07	52.7	+73	31	A 064	10	09.5	+58	28
A 030	07	52.9	+72	03	A 065	10	13.5	+38	39
A 031	07	53.7	+74	19	A 066	10	13.6	+38	45
A 032	07	54.1	+74	25	A 067	10	13.7	+38	41
A 033	07	59.0	+59	07	A 068	10	15.8	+43	48
A 034	07	59.1	+59	09	A 069	10	16.9	+60	18
035	08	09.4	+57	47	A 070	10	21.0	+25	31

Catalogue

SECTION 3: ANONYMOUS GALAXY CO-ORDINATES FOR EPOCH 2000.0 (cont'd).

W.S. No.	R.A.	Dec.	W.S. No.	R.A.	Dec.
A 071	10h 22.5m	+57° 02'	A 106	11h 51.4m	+35° 14'
A 072	10 22.1	+38 30	A 107	12 07.8	+67 24
A 073	10 22.4	+38 35	A 108	12 16.2	+28 09
A 074	10 22.3	+22 26	A 109	12 28.2	+44 27
A 075	10 22.7	+19 26	A 110	12 51.0	+47 42
A 076	10 23.7	+33 46	A 111	12 52.9	+10 00
A 077	10 27.0	+28 39	A 112	12 54.7	+13 14
A 078	10 28.3	+22 35	A 113	12 56.4	+52 08
A 079	10 28.8	+26 21	A 114	12 56.5	+48 16
A 080	10 29.3	+26 05	A 115	12 58.3	+14 34
A 081	10 39.5	+47 57	A 116	13 01.8	+27 36
A 082	10 39.8	+47 56	A 117	13 02.1	+27 39
A 083	10 43.4	+40 48	A 118	13 02.1	+27 39
A 084	10 43.5	+39 42	A 119	13 04.0	+28 12
A 085	10 47.9	+28 16	A 120	13 11.5	+31 33
A 086	10 51.2	+27 52	A 121	13 30.1	+31 24
A 087	11 02.5	+16 44	A 122	13 30.3	+31 20
A 088	11 15.1	+31 02	A 123	13 34.7	+62 00
A 089	11 20.7	+31 14	A 124	13 37.7	+39 10
A 090	11 21.1	+31 15	A 125	14 01.9	+33 34
A 091	11 32.6	+52 58	A 126	14 03.7	+35 45
A 092	11 33.2	+63 18	A 127	14 09.4	+49 02
A 093	11 34.5	+71 33	A 128	14 10.1	+54 13
A 094	11 34.9	+54 39	A 129	14 27.4	+29 57
A 095	11 36.9	+55 10	A 130	14 29.1	+31 47
A 096	11 38.1	+58 46	A 131	14 29.1	+30 05
A 097	11 39.3	+58 17	A 132	14 37.7	+30 29
A 098	11 42.0	+32 01	A 133	15 40.2	+21 32
A 099	11 42.3	+16 02	A 134	16 27.6	+40 41
A 100	11 42.4	+18 20	A 135	16 28.4	+33 13
A 101	11 42.4	+20 08	A 136	16 28.6	+39 31
A 102	11 43.8	+19 59	A 137	16 28.7	+39 30
A 103	11 44.8	+20 08	A 138	16 30.3	+41 07
A 104	11 46.8	+14 33	A 139	16 30.6	+41 13
A 105	11 47.9	+56 00	A 140	16 31.0	+41 10

Catalogue

SECTION 3: ANONYMOUS GALAXY CO—ORDINATES FOR EPOCH 2000.0 (cont'd).

W.S. No.	R.A.		Dec.	
A 141	16h	40.5m	+39°	20'
A 142	16	40.5	+39	15
A 143	16	43.2	+42	11
A 144	16	46.7	+36	05
A 145	16	46.8	+34	10
A 146	16	46.9	+34	10
A 147	16	47.2	+40	15
A 148	16	49.1	+48	38
A 149	16	50.2	+55	23
A 150	16	50.4	+55	50
A 151	16	52.3	+55	55
A 152	17	15.3	+57	27
A 153	20	43.8	+80	10
A 154	21	31.7	+02	29
A 155	22	10.0	+41	01
A 156	22	16.8	+41	30
A 157	22	20.8	+33	19
A 158	22	21.1	+36	36
A 159	22	22.5	+36	13
A 160	22	23.0	+36	24
A 161	22	23.0	+35	51
A 162	22	38.4	+35	24
A 163	22	38.5	+35	21
A 164	22	38.6	+35	22
A 165	22	38.7	+35	21

PART THREE

APPENDICES

APPENDIX 1: FORMATION OF AN ANONYMOUS GALAXIES CLUB.

With this volume of the Webb Society Deep-Sky Observers Handbook we announce the formation of the Anonymous Galaxies Club. This branch of the Webb Society will act as a clearing house of information concerning anonymous galaxies. Its main purpose will be to assist observers with all phases of observing the faint objects, including any questions or problems they may have. This club will also act as the main source of new observations for inclusion in the updated versions of Handbook volumes 'Clusters of Galaxies' and 'Anonymous Galaxies'. Occasionally, new observations will be published in the Webb Society Quarterly Journal.

Observers are requested to standardize their reporting along the lines of the observing form at the end of this Appendix. The form is pretty much self-explanatory; however, there are a few points I would like to address. The anonymous galaxy may be listed under different 'names', depending upon which catalogue you are using; if the observer knows of more than one name applied to the object, all should be included. Under the heading 'Remarks' the observer should include all the visible characteristics of the object. Any bright nearby object, such as a bright star or NGC/IC object, should be mentioned, as should any unusual star patterns. These 'bright' or unusual star patterns should be mentioned regardless of whether they are actually in the field of view or just beyond it. The ease or difficulty of seeing the object needs to be mentioned, along with the ocular focal length or magnification which gave the best overall view of the object in question. In fact, any information the observer deems important should be included in the 'Remarks' section. If necessary, use another sheet of paper or the back of the observing form itself.

The finder charts should be used in the following manner. The Low Power circle is used as a reference field for locating the galaxy in question. All bright reference points should be included even if outside the field. The High Power circle should show the anonymous galaxy exactly as it appears, set against the stars in the immediate vicinity. Include the ocular focal length and/or magnification used for each field drawing. Also include the four directions N, S, E (f.), W (p.). Negative results, accompanied by a drawing indicating exactly where the object lies, should also be submitted; these help determine the minimum aperture required to see a particular object. Finally, it would be helpful if observers requiring a reply would send a stamped addressed envelope. Observers recording anonymous galaxies are encouraged to send their reports to: Webb Society Anonymous Galaxies Club, c/o Ronald J. Morales, 1440 S. Marmora, Tucson, Arizona 85713, U.S.A.

R.J.M.

ANONYMOUS GALAXY OBSERVER'S LOG

OBJECT NAME(S):_____

CATALOGUE(S) USED:_____

R.A.:_____ DEC.:_____ EPOCH:_____

SEEING:_____ TRANSPARENCY:_____

TELESCOPE:_____ f/ _____

OCULAR(S) USED & MAGNIFICATION:_____

DATE:_____ TIME (U.T.):_____

. . . .

FINDER CHART:

N.B. Include the primary directions, i.e., N, S, E (f.) and W (p.)

REMARKS:

N.B. Record any detail seen, such as mottling, shape, presence or absence of nucleus or central brightening, nearby objects, etc.

APPENDIX 2: BIBLIOGRAPHY

P. Nilson, 'Uppsala General Catalogue of Galaxies', 1973

B. Vorontsov-Velyaminov and A. Krasnogorskaja, 'Morphological Catalogue of Galaxies', 1962, 5 volumes

Webb Society, 'Webb Society Deep-Sky Observers Handbook', Volume 5: Clusters of Galaxies; Enslow, 1982.

F. Zwicky, 'Catalogue of Galaxies and Clusters·of Galaxies', 1961, 6 volumes

APPENDIX 3: SUGGESTED READING

R. J. Morales, 'Abell 347 Cluster of Galaxies', Sky and Telescope December 84, page 578

M. J. Thomson, 'Galaxy Cluster Around NGC 3158', Webb Society Quarterly Journal, April 83 (No. 52), page #17

M. J. Thomson, 'UO6527 A Group of Connected Galaxies', Webb Society Quarterly Journal, October 83 (No. 54), page 13